The F.E.A.R. of the Lord

VIRTUOUS WARRIORS

Other Bible Studies in the Virtuous Warriors Series

Rebekah's Confidence

A Virtuous Woman: The Fairytale Story

The F.E.A.R. of the Lord

Sharon Hoskins

Proverbs 31:30 Ministry
2011

Scripture quotations were taken from The Holy Bible, New King James Version copyright 1982 by Thomas Nelson, Inc.

ISBN: 978-0-9908245-0-3

Proverbs 31:30 Ministry

www.proverbs3130ministry.com

proverbs3130ministries@gmail.com

Edited by Shayla Soehrmann

Virtuous Warriors design by Kristi Johnson

Sharon Hoskins is a wife and mother of two young children. She is the director of women's ministry at her church and teaches the ladies Sunday school class. She is the author of Bible studies and retreat workshops. Sharon holds a BS in Communication. As a gifted encourager, she speaks to women through God's word and her own Christian journey. She is an advocate for mentoring programs and encourages all women to find a mentor and become a mentor. Every Friday at noon she hosts a live radio show with her friend and mentor, Janie Ratzlaff. She is the founder of Proverbs 31:30 Ministry and desires to encourage and equip women to be all God created them to be. She is passionate about providing practical tools for women to live confident in Christ and find a fulfilling relationship with the Father. More information can be found at proverbs3130ministry.com

Contents

Acknowledgements

To my husband, Terry, for all his love and support, for fixing things when I break them, for making my work environment appealing, and for taking up my slack when I stop to write.

I love you.

Preface

This study came together in 2008, as I was praying about a ladies retreat for the fall. God encouraged me to take a look at the verse that Proverbs 31:30 Ministry stands on, *"Charm is deceitful and beauty is passing, but a woman who fears the Lord, she shall be praised."* As I read the verse, I realized that the term "the fear of the Lord" is used in so many different ways and can be confusing to believers, both new and old. So I began to dig into the Scriptures to find out all I could about the fear of the Lord. It became very clear that I had never really understood the term myself and had never heard it explained in the way God was revealing to me. *"Blessed is every one who fears the Lord, who walks in His ways. When you eat the labor of your hands, you shall be happy, and it shall be well with you. Your wife shall be like a fruitful vine in the very heart of your house, your children like olive plants all around your table. Behold, thus shall the man be blessed who fears the Lord."* Psalm 128:1-4. These are promises given only to those who fear the Lord. If we want to receive them in our lives, we must know what it means to fear the Lord.

Many people have an unhealthy fear of God that puts them in bondage to rituals and laws. *"Therefore the Lord says, 'Inasmuch as these people draw near with their mouths and honor Me with their lips, but have removed their hearts far from Me, and their fear toward Me is taught by the commandments of men'."* Isaiah 29:13. These commandments of men do not bring us into a relationship with the Father, but into a relationship with men because of their rules. People are most likely to associate with those who have the same interests, moral values, and religious views because they play by the same rules of life. Some rules that we follow are taught by God and some rules are taught by men. Either way, we all follow some sort of guideline for our lives. We make choices and decisions based on our rules of life. *"If you fear the Lord and serve Him and obey His voice, and do not rebel against the commandment of the Lord, then both you and the king who reigns over you will continue following the Lord your God. However, if you do not obey the voice of the Lord, but rebel against the commandment of the Lord, then the hand of the Lord will be against you, as it was against your fathers."* 1 Samuel 12:14-15. *"But it will not be well with the wicked; nor will he prolong his days, which are as a shadow, because he does not fear before God."* Ecclesiastes 8:13.

Some people do not fear the Lord at all. If we understand that the fear of the Lord is about a relationship with Him, it will help us understand how people can live without fear, because they live without a relationship. When we know that, then we should have enough compassion to share Christ with them. All of these Scripture were very eye opening and helped me understand the depth of what the term "the fear of the

Lord" really meant so; I put together a weekend study for the retreat. The ladies said it was more like a conference than a retreat because we were studying the entire weekend, but we all learned so much about the fear of the Lord, I decided to use it as an outline and expand it to a Bible Study that many could enjoy. I pray that as you take the time to work through this study, it will help you grow closer to the Father in a relationship. I pray you will be encouraged to receive correction, instruction, and guidance and that you will gain wisdom and understanding of the fear of the Lord.

Introduction

The purpose of this study is to dig into what God says about the fear of the Lord. We will find many Scriptures that will help us understand a more in-depth meaning. We will find how the fear of the Lord can bless our life, strengthen our body, give us health, and make us wise. *The F.E.A.R. of the Lord* is set up as an acronym to bring a fullness of all that the fear of the Lord can bring into our lives. "F" is about our Faithful Fellowship to the Father in heaven. This section will deal with prayer, which will include how to pray and when to pray. It will deal with Bible study how to evaluate your Bible and hear God through it. It will also deal with how faithful we are to spend time with God and how faithful we are to spend time with His people. "E" is our Expressions of Exaltations to the Father. In every relationship, we express how we feel with our words and actions. Expressions of love and gratitude should be heard by God and seen by others. We can exalt God by living for Him in our everyday life and testifying of His greatness to those around us. This shows a consistent lifestyle. "A" is our Attitude to Apply His teachings. Application is our obedience to God. Our attitude toward God is seen in how well we listen and obey His commands. An attitude can be good or bad, attractive or ugly and whichever one we display to people is the one we display to God. Obeying with a bad attitude usually means we are just following rules without love. Obeying with a good attitude usually means that we are willing to obey because of respect and love for God. Our attitude in obedience is very important in our relationship with Him. "R" is Recognition to Reverence. We must recognize God for who He is, what He says, and how He works to revere Him. This section will show you how to recognize God's voice, His actions, and His people.

The goal of this study is to bring a better understanding of the fear of the Lord. It has been explained away with simple definitions. Some have said that it is like the honor and respect that you have for your earthly father. Others have said that you shouldn't fear Him as the boogieman, but as your Creator. Understanding the fear of the Lord is not easy when the explanations are so vague. It is more than just honor and respect; it's about a relationship with our Father. It's about intimacy with our Creator. It's about love beyond the flesh, joy without words, and peace that surpasses understanding. To walk in the fear of the Lord should be a delight to us as it was for Jesus. The question of "WWJD" (What Would Jesus Do) can be answered in this study. He was faithful to fellowship with His Father. *"So He Himself often withdrew into the wilderness and prayed."* Luke 5:16. He exalted His Father in everything, from Matthew 4:4, *"Man shall not live by bread alone, but by every word that proceeds from the mouth of God"* to John 19:11 *"You could have no power at all against Me unless it had been given you from above."* He had an attitude of obedience to His Father, *"And being found in appearance as a man, He*

(Jesus) *humbled Himself and became obedient to the point of death, even the death of the cross."* Philippians 2:8. He recognized who His Father was and what His Father said, *"My doctrine is not Mine, but His who sent Me."* John 7:16. So, what would Jesus do? He would delight in the fear of the Lord, *"His delight is in the fear of the Lord."* Isaiah 11:3. As you learn what it means, and how to grow in it, may your delight also be in the fear of the Lord.

Truth

Truth is very important in our Christian walk. When we have truth, we have life, it makes us free, and we can grow up in all things.

Jesus said to him, "I am the way, the truth, and the life. No one comes to the Father except through Me."
John 14:6

"And you shall know the truth, and the truth shall make you free."

John 8:32

"...speaking truth in love may grow up in all things into Him who is the head – Christ – from whom the whole body, joined and knit together by what every joint supplies, according to the effective working by which every part does its share, causes growth of the body for the edifying of itself in love."
Eph. 4:15-16

We will find that "the fear of the Lord" is used collectively as one word throughout Scripture. It is used as a noun in Proverbs 1:7, *"The fear of the Lord is the beginning of knowledge, but fools despise wisdom and instruction."* It is used as a verb in Proverbs 3:7-8, *"Do not be wise in your own eyes; fear the Lord and depart from evil. It will be health to your flesh, and strength to your bones."* Much of God's word expresses its importance and Proverbs is full of its benefits. We can see by these few scriptures that we are hindered from knowledge, health, strength, and wisdom when we do not fear the Lord. *"My people are destroyed for lack of knowledge. Because you have rejected knowledge, I also will reject you from being priest for me; because you have forgotten the law of your God, I also will forget your children."* Hosea 4:6. *"For I desire mercy and not sacrifice, and the knowledge of God more than burnt offerings."* Hosea 6:6. It is important to God that we obtain knowledge and wisdom. According to Scripture, the fear of the Lord is first, and then we gain knowledge, understanding, and wisdom. *"Oh, how great is Your goodness, which You have laid up for those who fear You."* Psalm 31:19. There is goodness stored up for the ones that will choose the fear of the Lord. The goodness stored up for them is not money, cars, houses, or possessions. The goodness stored up is gladness, welfare, and joy which describes some of the fruit of the Spirit. (Galatians 5:22-25) *"Let all the earth fear the Lord; let all the inhabitants of the world stand in awe of Him."* Psalm 33:8. *"Behold, the eye of the Lord is on those who fear Him, on those who hope in His mercy."* Psalm 33:18.

Read Proverbs 1:20-32 and answer the questions below.

What is the warning in this passage? _____
_____
_____

What are the consequences of this decision? _____
_____
_____

Knowledge of God comes from the fear of the Lord. Notice that verse 22 of Proverbs 1 says that fools hate knowledge. Verse 29 shows that those who hate knowledge do not choose the fear of the Lord. If we will repent when God corrects, then He will pour out His Spirit on you and give you wisdom. This passage of Scripture shows us how much God wants to give to us and longs for us to hear Him. He calls aloud and cries out to all, but who will listen?

Read Proverbs 1:33-2:11 and answer the questions below.

What must you do before understanding the fear of the Lord? _____

_____

_____

What benefits come as a result? _____

_____

_____

From Proverbs 1:20 to 2:11, we can see two choices and the consequences of each one. The Bible is full of the word "if", which emphasizes our free will to choose the paths in our life. This is why it is so important for us to know what the Bible says so we know how to make decisions in our life. If we choose the fear of the Lord, we will find many benefits to help us in our Christian life. The definition of fear is to honor, respect, revere, and worship. This definition is summed up in Matthew 22:37-38, *"You shall love the Lord your God with all your heart, with all your soul, and with all your mind. This is the first and great commandment."* When we love the Lord this way, we have a healthy fear of the Lord. Without this fear, we will not follow the commands of Christ in a consistent way of life. We will compromise because of our own wants and desires. There must be a fear instilled in us out of love for our Father. How do we show our love to God? Jesus said in John 14:21, *"He who has My commandments and keeps them, it is he who loves Me. And he who loves Me will be loved by My Father, and I will love him and manifest Myself to him."* He also states in 23, *"If anyone loves Me, he will keep My word; and My Father will love him, and We will come to him and make Our home with him."* The fear we should have for the Lord is one of respect and love. Not fear that He will hurt us when we don't do what He says, but that we do what He says because of the love we have for Him. People say all the time, "God loves you" this is true, He displayed His love at the Cross. The question is; how much do you really love God? Will you give your life for Him? Will you obey Him even at the cost of yourself? If you love Him, the Bible says that you will obey Him. Obedience isn't in just what we want to do; it's in everything He says to do. Love is the key to the fear of the Lord.

If we love the Lord, we will obey the second commandment that He gives us, *"Love your neighbor as yourself. On these two commandments hang all the Law and the Prophets."* Matthew 22:39-40. So the basic obedience of God is to love. Many of us try to love on our own, in our flesh, based on how we are treated, how we feel, and what we think because our love is conditional. The love that God requires us to love with is His love and it is unconditional. The Bible describes the love that God expects from us. *"Love suffers long and is kind; love does not envy; love does not parade itself, is not puffed up; does not behave rudely, does not seek its own, is not provoked, thinks no evil; does not rejoice in iniquity, but rejoices in the truth; bears all things, believes all things, hopes all things, endures all things. Love never fails."* 1 Corinthians 13:4-8. If we love our spouse this way, we should have a great marriage. This love cannot be imitated in our flesh because it will only last a season. It is a lifestyle, and without this lifestyle of love, we do not know God. *"He who does not love does not know God, for God is love."* 1 John 4:8. If we are successful in this love, the Holy Spirit dwells in us, and we are well on our way to understanding the fear of the Lord because the love that we have from God is a pure love. *"And we have known and believed the love that God has for us. God is love, and he who abides in love abides in God, and God in him."* 1 John 4:16.

Love is the reason Jesus went to the cross. *"For God so loved the world that He gave His only begotten Son, that whoever believes in Him should not perish but have everlasting life."* John 3:16. This is a description of how much He loves us, but how much do we love Him? *"For this is the love of God, that we keep His commandments. And His commandments are not burdensome."* 1 John 5:3. This study can give you all the information needed to understand the fear of the Lord, but without love it will just be another set of laws and rituals added to your list. The only way you can love with God's love is to receive Jesus Christ as your Lord and Savior. *"If you confess with your mouth the Lord Jesus and believe in your heart that God has raised Him from the dead, you will be saved. For with the heart one believes to righteousness, and with the mouth confession is made to salvation."* Romans 10:9-10. *"Whoever keeps His word, truly the love of God is perfected in him. By this we know that we are in Him."* 1 John 2:5. God's love can be perfected in us if we allow Jesus to become our Lord as well as our Savior. God has already done everything for us, what will we give Him in return? He is only asking for your love back to Him.

Read 1 John 5:1-5 and answer the questions below.

What do you read about those who are born of God? _____
_____

What do you read about love? _____
_____

What does 1 John 5:18 say? _____
_____
_____

We can keep the commandments of God, we can overcome difficulties of this world, and we can be strengthened in the faith, it all depends on how much we believe, and our belief will be seen in our commitment.

Chapter 2 ~ Relationship

The fear of the Lord is a relationship that begins with love. When you receive Jesus Christ as your Lord and Savior, it is the beginning of a beautiful relationship. When you say the prayer for salvation, you have just been introduced to Jesus Christ and now you can have a relationship with the Father. Then, like all relationships, it must be nurtured by you. Many people have walked away from God because they did not know how to build their relationship. They said a prayer and did not understand what else to do. Some have been told that God would fix all their problems, so they only call on Him when they have one. Some have been told that all they have to do is say a prayer, live as they want, and they will still go to heaven, so their prayer is a "get out of hell free" card. Others have been told that they would start doing things right when they say a prayer because God was their leader now, so they throw their noses in the air and glorify themselves. The truth is that the prayer of salvation opens the door to a relationship with the Father, through the Son. If you don't go in the door of Christ and build the relationship, then what are you waiting for?

Through the precious blood of Jesus, we are able to come to the Father. Jesus said, *"I am the way, the truth and the life. No one comes to the Father except through Me."* John 14:6. The first step to understanding the fear of the Lord is to evaluate your own salvation. Has what you've been taught about salvation been described in this Chapter? If so, make sure your salvation is secure with God. Some denominations are preaching that repentance is not necessary anymore, however, Jesus said, *"Repent, for the kingdom of heaven is at hand."* Matthew 4:17. Peter said in Acts 3:19, *"Repent therefore and be converted, that your sins may be blotted out, so that times of refreshing may come from the presence of the Lord."* Paul said in Acts 26:20, *"...that they should repent, turn to God, and do works befitting repentance."* Where in the Bible did it change if repentance is not necessary anymore? Hebrews 13:8-9, *"Jesus Christ is the same yesterday, today, and forever. Do not be carried about* (away) *with various and strange doctrines."* Denominations have many doctrines, so be sure yours lines up with God's holy word. Repentance is necessary for salvation.

What does 2 Peter 3:9 say? _____
_____
_____

What did Jesus say in Revelation 2:5 to the church of Ephesus? _____
_____
_____

What did He say to the church of Pergamos in Revelation 2:16? _____

_____

_____

What did He say to the church of Thyatira in Revelation 2:21-23? _____

_____

_____

What did He say to the church of Sardis in Revelation 3:3? _____

_____

_____

As you can see, there is a consistency of repentance to each church, which had something different to repent of. After each time He told them to repent, He then encouraged them to overcome, to be faithful, hold fast, and to keep His works. Jesus said in Revelation 3:19, *"As many as I love, I rebuke and chasten (discipline). Therefore be zealous (eager) and repent."* We do the same thing to our children when they do wrong. When we discipline them for something, we then want them to understand what they did wrong, and stop doing it, that's repentance. Why is it that we want our children to do what we tell them to do, when we tell them to do it, but we don't give God the same respect we expect from our children? Repentance is to stop doing what is wrong in the sight of God and does not end with our salvation prayer. We will continue to repent for things we do wrong as baby Christians and mature. It is a way of life for a believer.

Some Christians are adopting the idea that God gives blessings of this earth to fix your problems or to bless His children. We have all heard it, "Give a hundred dollars to this ministry, and God will give you a thousand in return." "Sow a seed of a thousand dollars and reap a harvest!" Books are being sold now that gives you instructions on how to make God give to you. The author of these lies will answer to God for their deception. The Bible gives a warning to us about those who twist scripture. *"Therefore, beloved, looking forward to these things, be diligent to be found by Him in peace, without spot and blameless; and consider that the longsuffering of our Lord is salvation – as also our beloved brother Paul, according to the wisdom given to him, has written to you, as also in all his epistles, speaking in them of these things hard to understand, which untaught and unstable people twist to their own destruction, as they do also the rest of the Scriptures. You therefore, beloved, since you know this beforehand, beware lest you also fall from your own steadfastness, being led away with the error of the wicked; but grow in the grace and knowledge of our Lord and Savior Jesus Christ. To Him be the glory both now and forever. Amen."* 2 Peter 3:15-18. People are taking Scripture out of context, twisting it, and not only destroying themselves, but taking others with them. Hopefully you are still reading this study even if a nerve has been hit. If you will stick it out, we will dig into some Scriptures that will bring out the fullness of what is being said. Consistency is a must with God's word and it will not contradict itself. *"Be diligent to present yourself approved to God, a worker who does not need to be ashamed, rightly dividing the word of truth."* 2 Timothy 2:15. It is very important to "rightly divide" God's word, to not twist Scripture, and to grow in the grace and knowledge of Jesus.

So, let's start with, *"Give and it will be given to you; good measure, pressed down, shaken together, and running over will be put into your bosom. For with the same measure that you use, it will be measured back to you."* Luke 6:38. This verse cannot be plucked out of the Bible and attached to money or stuff. It has to be used within the context of the Scriptures. Go back to the beginning of what is being taught. You can go back as far as 6:20 to find the beginning of the teaching. We are going to 6:35 just to get the understanding. *"But love your enemies, do good, and lend, hoping for nothing in return; and your reward will be great, and you will be sons of the Most High. For He is kind to the unthankful and evil. Therefore be merciful, just as your Father also is merciful. Judge not, and you will not be judged. Condemn not, and you shall not be condemned. Forgive and you will be forgiven."* Luke 6:35-37. There is nothing about money, treasures, or earthy possessions in these verses. You should give to others as you have been given to by God. God gave you His Son because He loved you before you loved Him, 1 John 4:10, so love others and you will receive more love in return. Give mercy just as God was merciful to you and more mercy will be given to you as you give it. Forgive others as God the Father has forgiven you. How can we justify taking this Scripture and making it about anything of this earth? Jesus said, *"Do not lay up for yourselves treasures on earth, where moth and rust destroy and where thieves break in and steal; but lay up for yourselves treasures in heaven, where neither moth nor rust destroys and where thieves do not break in and steal. For where your treasure is there your heart will be also."* Matthew 6:19-21. The only one found in Scripture promising anything of this earth is Satan in, *"Again, the devil took Him up on an exceedingly high mountain, and showed Him all the kingdoms of the world and their glory. And he said to Him, 'All these things I will give You if You will fall down and worship me."* Matthew 4:8-9. If he did it to Jesus, don't you think he will do it to you?

Read James 5:1-8 and answer the questions below.

What does it say about the people and their riches? _____

_____

_____

_____

What does it say brethren should do? _____

_____

_____

We seem to want all the privileges of God, but none of the responsibilities. *"If you endure chastening God deals with you as with sons; for what son is there whom a father does not chasten? But if you are without chastening of which all have become partakers, then you are illegitimate and not sons."* Hebrews 12:7-8. Chastening is discipline, which is correction. That means you will not get your way all the time and you have to change your ways to be more like His. God is a Father to us, not a royal King who spoils His kids with everything they want. God promises to supply our every need according to His riches in glory, Philippians 4:19 and glory is full of spiritual riches not earthly ones. Jesus gives us a warning, *"Take heed that no one deceives you."* Matthew 24:4. It is more important that you not be deceived than to obtain riches.

Read Matthew 24:4-13 and answer the questions below.

Verse eight says, "All these are the beginning of sorrows." What are "these"? ____

_____

_____

_____

In verse nine, who is "you" referring to?" _____

When people get offended, the first thing they do is betray the one who offended them. It begins with talking about them to others and then it turns to hatred. Many get offended at the teachings of Jesus. He had many of His disciples turn from following Him because they were offended. (Read John 6:60-66). Some of you may be offended right now at this study, if so, ask God to show you why. The Scriptures are God's word and if you are offended by it, then your problem is with God. Ask Him to soften your heart to receive His word.

Why is it so important to receive His word? (Hint: vs. 11) _____

_____

_____

What will lawlessness (sin) cause in our life if we allow it to continue? _____

_____

_____

What must we do, according to verse 13? _____

_____

_____

This is why it is so important for us to be disciplined children. He disciplines us because He loves us. We have translated love as acceptance without change. In today's society, everyone wants to be accepted just as the way they are, even if they are disrespectful, unloving, unforgiving, mean, and hateful. People don't want to take responsibility for the decisions they make, or be held accountable to follow through with their commitments. The golden rule, treat others the way you want to be treated, is not displayed anymore. It is more likely that we are treating others the way we don't want to be treated. Those who cry for mercy the most, are the least likely to give it in return. We don't honor, respect, or value the people in our lives, but we want to be honored, respected, and valued. Everything is one-sided and we treat God the same way. We say that God loves us and we tell others that He loves them, but do you love God? When is the last time you asked someone that question? "Do you love God?" Jesus said, *"If you keep My commandments, you will abide in My love, just as I have kept My Father's commandments and abide in His love."* in John 15:10. But because we have defined love as acceptance, we don't understand God's love. We want God to accept us just as we are, and He does, but to be His child we must also accept and obey the rules of His house. That means we will change as He corrects and instructs us in His ways. God will not honor those who do not receive His correction or bless those that do not accept His instruction. Christianity is not a feel good lifestyle. It is one of discipline, commitment, obedience, and love.

In a relationship, communication is a must, but we don't talk to our neighbor to get to know our spouse. It is important that we understand the "communication system" so we know who to talk to when we spend time in our relationship. The Father, Son and Holy Spirit are all three God, so when we pray, we pray to God, not understanding the channels of communication. When we speak to God, we are communicating with all three, just in different ways. Each Godhead of the Trinity has a position working in unity for the whole. John 1:1-2 says, *"In the beginning was the Word, and the Word was with God, and the Word was God. He was in the beginning with God."* If the Bible you are reading does not acknowledge Jesus' deity in these verses, then throw it away.

Jesus is the Word.

What does John 1:14 say. _____
_____
_____
_____

The Holy Spirit proceeds from the Father.

What does John 15:26 say? _____
_____
_____
_____

Even though they are all three God, they are in different positions. Jesus is at the right hand of the Father, making intercession for us. *"It is Christ who died, and furthermore is also risen, who is even at the right hand of God, who also makes intercession for us."* Romans 8:34. *"Through the resurrection of Jesus Christ, who has gone into heaven and is at the right hand of God, angels and authorities and powers having been made subject to Him."* 1 Peter 3:21b-22. *"Therefore He is also able to save to the uttermost those who come to God through Him, since he ever lives to make intercession for them."* Hebrews 7:25.

Read 2 Corinthians 5:17-19 and answer the questions below.

What is the stipulation for things to become new in verse 17? _____
_____
_____

How are we reconciled to God according to verse 18? _____
_____
_____
_____

Jesus is our High Priest. He sympathizes with our weaknesses, and He will give us mercy and grace to help us when we come to Him, (Hebrews 4:14-16). He is the author of eternal salvation to all who obey Him, (Hebrews 5:9). *"We have such a High Priest, who is seated at the right hand of the throne of the Majesty in the heavens,"* Hebrews 8:1. Jesus died on the cross to reconcile us back to the Father. Through Him, God sees us as clean, so we can have a relationship with the Father. This is why we pray in Jesus' name. It's only through His obedience, His sacrifice, and His blood that we are made righteous.

The Holy Spirit is given to those that accept Jesus as their Lord and Savior to help them. John 16:13 says that the Holy Spirit will guide you into all truth. *"But the Helper, the Holy Spirit, whom the Father will send in My name, He will teach you all things, and bring to your remembrance all things that I said to you."* John 14:26. The Holy Spirit gives us the ability to hear God speak to our hearts in prayer, in a message, in Bible Study, in a song, etc.

Read 1 Corinthians 2:9-14 and answer the questions below.

What does it say about the Spirit of God? _____
_____
_____
_____

What is a benefit of the Spirit of God according to verse 12? _____
_____
_____

What does the Holy Spirit do according to verse 13? _____
_____
_____

Why can "natural man" not receive the Holy Spirit according to verse 14? _____
_____
_____

What does 1 Corinthians 3:16 say. _____
_____
_____
_____

Read Ephesians 2:11-22 and answer the questions below.

What does it say about us without Christ? _____
_____
_____
_____

What does it say has reconciled us to the Father? _____
_____
_____
_____

What does it say about the Spirit in these Scriptures? _____
_____
_____
_____

What does it say about Jesus in these Scriptures? _____
_____
_____
_____

The Holy Spirit is in us if we have received Jesus as our Lord and Savior. *"And I will pray the Father, and He will give you another Helper, that He may abide with you forever, even the Spirit of truth, whom the world cannot receive, because it neither sees Him nor knows Him; but you know Him, for He dwells with you and will be in you."* John 14:16-17. *"The love of God has been poured out in our hearts by the Holy Spirit who was given to us."* Romans 5:5. It is important that we remember who we are talking to when we pray. The Father hears us because of Jesus and the blood He shed at Calvary. We hear the Father because of the Holy Spirit living inside of us. It all works together in the relationship with God.

Love

Love is the reason we have a relationship with the Father. He loved us so much that He gave His Son. He desires our love in return.

"For God so loved the world that He gave His only begotten Son, that whoever believes in Him should not perish but have everlasting life."

John 3:16

"You shall love the Lord your God with all your heart, with all your soul, with all your strength, and with all your mind, and your neighbor as yourself."

Luke 10:27

"Beloved, let us love one another, for love is of God; and everyone who loves is born of God and knows God. He who does not love does not know God, for God is love."
1 John 4:7-8

Fellowship requires faithfulness in prayer. Fellowship is one of many words used to describe talking. It is used mostly when we are referring to getting together with other believers. Communication is used when we are referring to our family. Visiting is used when we are referring to our friends. Speaking is used when we are referring to business relations, and prayer is used when we are referring to God. These are all words used for talking to different people in different relationships. Prayer is talking to God. So many people do not know what it means to pray, how to pray, or when to pray. Some of us were taught rhyming prayers as children and in return taught it to our own. These "prayers" are recited like a jingle and become a ritual of words said without meaning or feeling, therefore, not really speaking to anyone about anything. We become faithful to the prayer, always reciting before a meal or before going to sleep, but not to the One we say we are praying to. To be faithful to God, we must have a relationship with God. We are not faithful to people we do not know, so to be faithful to God, we must know Him. Our commitment or faithfulness to others is based on our communication level in the relationship and the same is true with God. As our relationship is nurtured with prayer, and grows with Bible study, it increases our faith in Him and His word. Communication is the only way to get to know someone and build a relationship with that person. So, to build a relationship with the Father, we must know how to fellowship with Him in prayer.

How to Pray

This does not mean we will learn how to recite prayers of any sort. The prayer of Jabez is his own prayer. When Solomon prayed, he didn't recite his father David's prayers and when we pray, we shouldn't recite someone else's prayer either. Prayers are our own conversations with God and should be spoken from our own heart. When the disciples asked Jesus to teach them to pray, He instructed them to pray a certain way. We find the model prayer in Matthew 6:9-13 and Luke 11:2-4. Write out each verse below.

In this prayer, we find Reverence and Honor, verse 9. _____

_____

_____

In this prayer, we find Surrendered Control, verse 10. _____

_____

_____

_____

In this prayer, we find Provisions, verse 11. _____

_____

_____

_____

In this prayer, we find Repentance and Mercy, verse 12. _____

_____

_____

_____

In this prayer, we find Guidance and Protection, verse 13._____

_____

_____

_____

And this prayer is ended just as it began, with Reverence and Honor.

Jesus did not instruct the disciples to pray to Him or to the Holy Spirit, but to the Father in heaven with an attitude of respect, surrender, dependence, trust, humility, and love. The words used to express this attitude are up to the person themselves according to their relationship with the Father. Many say that they don't know how to pray, but if we pray our heart to God, without the rules man has put on prayer, then talking to God is pretty simple. When our heart is surrendered, dependent, humble, and full of love for God, then it will come out when we pray. *"A good man out of the good treasure of his heart brings forth good; and an evil man out of the evil treasure of his heart brings forth evil. For out of the abundance of the heart his mouth speaks."* Luke 6:45. If we have good in our heart toward God, then good will come out of our mouth to God. Prayer is not complicated; it is simply sharing our heart with the Father. *"Blessed are the pure in heart, for they shall see God."* Matthew 5:8. When our heart is pure before God, we will see Him, in our relationship with Him.

When to Pray

1 Thessalonians 5:17 says, *"pray without ceasing,"* and Ephesians 6:18 says, *"praying always with all prayer and supplication in the Spirit, being watchful to this end with all perseverance and supplication for all the saints."* Praying always without ceasing does not mean that we do nothing else, but pray. It means that we look to God throughout the day about everything we do and every decision we make. *"Trust in the Lord with all your heart, and lean not on your own understanding; in all your ways acknowledge Him, and He shall direct your paths."* Proverbs 3:5-6. This is how we are able to make choices in our life based on God's truth, when we allow Him to guide us by His Holy Spirit as we communicate

to Him in prayer. Constant communication or continual prayer is simply making God a part of your entire day, all your decisions, expectations, hurts, frustrations, and disappointments. From the time we get up to the time we go to bed we have conversations that go on in our head. We talk to ourselves about what we need to do and where we need to go. We discuss with ourselves people and situations that are happening in our lives. We can get so caught up in our own thoughts that sometimes we don't even hear the things that are going on around us. We have constant communication with ourselves, and if we practice, we can make God a part of those conversations, discussions, and thoughts. The trouble we have with this is that we are used to doing all the talking and it is important that we listen and give time for God to speak. Sometimes we get tired of talking to ourselves, so we pick up the phone or go to the computer to include someone else in our conversations, this still excludes God. Continual prayer will take practice, but it can be achieved if we try. It is really all about "the want to". If we want to do something, we will work to make it happen. How much do we really want God to be a part of our life? If we want it, we'll work hard and practice.

Read Isaiah 40:28-31 and answer the questions below.

What hope do you find here for your life? _____
_____
_____
_____

What is the one thing required of you? _____
_____
_____

We must understand that God gives us free will. He does not force anything on us. This is why "if" is mentioned so many times in the Bible, because there is always a choice to make. Each day of our life, we make a choice on how we will live, and if we will "trust in the Lord," if we will "wait on the Lord," and if we will "obey the Lord". If we do these things, then we will receive the promises to follow. It is amazing to see the number of people that claim the promises without following the "if". He cannot direct our path if we are not acknowledging Him in all our ways. He cannot direct our path if we don't trust Him above ourselves. The promises are for those that do what God says. We will know what He says if we are listening. *"In quietness and confidence shall be your strength."* Isaiah 30:15. The Lord is our strength and our confidence, "if". As we fellowship with Him, we learn more about Him and His promises to us. The more we learn, the more we believe; the more we believe, the more we trust; and the more we trust, the more our faith is increased. Being faithful to Him means that we believe Him, trust Him, and therefore we obey Him.

This obedience takes us back to love. *"For this is the love of God, that we keep His commandments. And His commandments are not burdensome. For whatever is born of God overcomes the world. And this is the victory that has overcome the world – our faith."* 1 John 5:3-4

Read Hebrews 11:1-12:2 and answer the questions below.

What is the definition of faith in Hebrews 11:1? _____

_____

_____

What does Hebrews 11:2 say that we obtain by faith? _____

_____

_____

According to Hebrews 11:3, God created the worlds by His word. He made visible what was invisible. How is this understood by us? _____

_____

According to Hebrews 11:4, what made Abel righteous? _____

_____

_____

According to Hebrews 11:5, why was Enoch taken away? _____

_____

_____

What does Hebrews 11:6 say about faith. _____

What can we obtain through faith just as Noah did in Hebrews 11:7? _____

_____

_____

What four things did Abraham do by faith according to Hebrews 11:8-10? _____

_____

_____

What rightful judgment did Sarah make that helped her have faith in Hebrews 11:11? _____

_____

According to Hebrews 11:12-13, what were they assured of? _____

What did they embrace? _____

Did they receive them by faith? _____

What did they confess? _____

According to Hebrews 11:14-16, why was God not ashamed to be called their God?
_____
_____

According to Hebrews 11:17-19, what was needed for Abraham to obey God? ____
_____
_____

According to Hebrews 11:20-22, what was needed to be successful in what was done? _____
_____
_____

Who had faith in Hebrews 11:23 in spite of the king's command? _____
_____
_____

Who chose affliction over comfort and the riches of Christ over the treasures of the world, in Hebrews 11:24-26? _____
_____
_____

What did Moses have to do in order to exercise his faith in Hebrews 11:27-29? ___
_____
_____

According to Hebrews 11:30-31, what was needed to have victory and salvation? _
_____
_____

What nine things are listed in Hebrews 11:32-34 that were done by faith? _____
_____
_____
_____

What kinds of things were endured in Hebrews 11:35-38 by faith? _____
_____

What does Hebrews 11:39 say was obtained by faith? _____
_____
_____

What has God provided for us according to Hebrews 11:40? _____
_____
_____

What instruction does Hebrews 12:1 give? _____
_____
_____

What encouragement do we find in Hebrews 12:2? _____
_____

Our faith in Christ, the Son of God, reconciles us back to the Father, and gives us a relationship with Him. In that relationship, we find love, which increases our faith and by our faith, we overcome the world. (1 John 5:3-4) This again shows us how important it is to fellowship with the Father through prayer. Prayer is the one area of our lives, as Christians, that we throw out there as if everyone should know how to do it, even if a person just got saved. We don't teach baby Christians to pray, but we tell them, 'it's a must.' So, we have churches full of people not knowing how to pray, therefore, not growing in a relationship with God. Those who have a healthy prayer life will have healthy fruit being produced in their life. Love, joy, peace, kindness, goodness, faithfulness, gentleness, longsuffering, and self-control are evident in their life because their relationship with God is healthy and strong. Our best example of a healthy and strong relationship with God is Jesus. Let's examine Jesus' relationship with the Father through His prayer life.

What evidence do we find in Luke 2:51-52 of Jesus' prayer life at the age of 12? __
_____

Why did Jesus tell us to pray? (Hint: Matthew 26:41) _____
_____

Where did Jesus pray? (Hint: Luke 6:12, Mark 1:35) _____

Where did Jesus tell us to pray? (Hint: Matthew 6:1-8) _____

How did Jesus pray? (Hint: John 17:1-26 and Matthew 26:39-54) _____
_____

How did Jesus tell us to pray? (Hint: Matthew 6:9-13) _____

How is this kind of prayer life achieved? _____
_____

What is keeping you from having the same kind of relationship as Jesus did with the Father? _____
_____

What is taking up your time and focus? _____
_____

Are the things taking up your time, wants, or needs? _____
_____

What can you do to change the focus of your time? _____
_____
_____

Ask God what He wants you to lay aside for Him. This may change as you grow, so continue to ask these questions because this is about how to find a deep, intimate, and personal relationship with the Father. We have been so churched that sometimes we are guilty of only spending time with God when it is convenient for us. God is worthy to be praised! How often do we really praise Him though? Is it only on Sundays because we have God penciled in on that day? Think about how we would feel if God acknowledged us only on a certain day or listened to our prayers only one day a week. We wouldn't feel that we were important to Him, would we? Let's put ourselves in God's place and think how we would like the treatment that we give. Sometimes if we turn the tables on our relationships, we don't really like the result that we get. It is amazing how the golden rule, treat others the way you want to be treated, is not practiced anymore. How we treat other relationships in our life is how we treat our relationship with God. If you take advantage of your friends, rebel against authority, or are selfish in any way in your relationships with others, then you probably take advantage of God, rebel against His authority, and seek only what you can receive from Him. God deserves more than any of us give Him, but examine yourself to see if you are guilty of dishonoring your relationship with Him. He has done everything possible to have a relationship with us. The Lord said, *"Behold, I stand at the door and knock. If anyone hears My voice and opens the door, I will come in to him and dine with him and he with Me."* Revelation 3:20. It is up to us to hear His voice, open the door, and let Him in. This goes beyond salvation to a relationship. Before salvation, He stood at the door and waited on us to acknowledge the knock. After salvation, we can find a relationship where He dines with us and us with Him, feasting on the bread of life, Jesus, who is the very word of God.

Fellowship requires faithfulness in Bible study. We tell Christians to read their Bible when they get born again, but very few are explaining how to read the Bible. Many people understand that to mean from cover to cover because that is how we understand reading. For those of us who can relate, we can't count the number of times we started Genesis 1:1. Most of us can probably quote it, but we gave up before we hardly got started because it was so overwhelming. We felt defeated because there was so much to read and learn that it seemed hopeless. Then we felt like a failure because no one told us that the Bible is not a typical book, and that it should not be read as if it were one. The Bible is the word of God. *"For the word of God is living and powerful, and sharper than any two-edged sword, piercing even to the division of soul and spirit, and of joints and morrow, and is a discerner of the thoughts and intents of the heart."* Hebrews 4:12. So, when we read the word of God, it is God speaking to us. It's living, it's powerful, and it will cut the junk out of our heart and fill us up with goodness when we receive what He says. This is why fellowship consists of prayer and Bible study; otherwise, our fellowship is all one-sided. We speak to God through prayer and He speaks to us through Bible Study. However, it is up to us to put forth the effort to both speak and hear.

What does Revelation 2:7 say. _____
_____

What does Revelation 2:11 say. _____
_____

What does Revelation 2:17 say. _____
_____

What does Revelation 2:29 say. _____
_____

What does Revelation 3:6 say. _____
_____

What does Revelation 3:13 say. _____
_____

What does Revelation 3:22 say. _____
_____

We have two ears and one mouth, but many times, we are so busy running our mouth that we can't hear anything that is said to us. Notice though that Jesus said, "He who has an ear..." Is He really talking about our physical ears? If so, then why didn't He say, "He who has ears," think for a moment, could He be talking about having a listening heart? A listening heart will be corrected and instructed. A listening heart will repent and surrender. A listening heart will gain wisdom and understanding. A listening heart will walk in the fear of the Lord.

Bible Study is an act of listening to God. However, we must be cautious of different interpretations. So many interpretations cause so many opinions and result in so many divisions. We must be careful that we are not allowing ourselves to be deceived because of conveniences. Information is given in the front of Bible versions to let us know how they have been interpreted. Some have taken the King James Version and written a new version from it. If the version was not taken from the original language then it is a watered down version. Turn your Bible to Romans 8:1, *"There is therefore now no condemnation to those who are in Christ Jesus, who do not walk according to the flesh, but according to the Spirit."* If your version stops at "Christ Jesus" then it has altered God's word. How many other mistakes could there be?

Read Matthew 4:6, Satan knows Scripture he just twists it. Satan can simplify Scripture to the point that we don't have to pray and trust God. We need to understand that some of the companies that are printing the Bible and interpreting it are not Christ-based. Satan has been counterfeiting God for thousands of years and this is just another way he can get into our life and deceive us from God's truth. Don't allow yourself to be lead astray for ease of reading. Just because it says, Holy Bible on the cover doesn't mean the contents are holy or those who interpreted it are holy. We should be willing to replace our Bible Version even if we find just one mistake because we love God more than our version. If we get off track, even a little bit, it could lead us away from God.

Read James 2:8-11 and answer the questions below.

What does it say about stumbling in one point? _____
_____
_____

What does it say about partiality? _____
_____
_____

Let us not compromise in any area of our life. If we have truly given our life to Christ, then the Holy Spirit will give us understanding when we read a version that is not watered down with conveniences. Just because we don't understand something, does not mean we need to run out and get a simplified version. Babies drink milk, then purified food, then solids. We would choke a baby if we put a piece of steak in its mouth and the same is true with God's word.

Read Hebrews 5:13-14 and answer the questions below.

What does it say about those who are babes in Christ? _____
_____

What does it say about those who are of full age? _____
_____

There is nothing wrong with being a babe in Christ; however, we should not want to stay babies. *"As newborn babes, desire the pure milk of the word, that you may grow thereby, if indeed you have tasted that the Lord is gracious."* 1 Peter 2:2. According to this Scripture, only the pure milk of the word will help us grow, not watered down milk. We will not understand some things because of our maturity level, but God will reveal them, as we are able to eat. The depth of God's word is immeasurable. Don't get discouraged if you don't understand everything you read. Be patient in prayer and content with what He gives and He will give us understanding as we need.

Fellowship requires faithfulness to surrender. Surrendering our life to God is more than just a salvation prayer; it is giving everything we have, think, want, and feel to Him. It is giving up our will for His will, our thinking for His thinking, and our desires for His desires. Many of us do not want to surrender because we think we will lose our identity. We are afraid to surrender because we want to keep control of our own destiny. We have this idea that we know what is best for our life, but the truth is God knows what is best for it. He has a perfect plan for us, but it takes our surrender to receive that perfect plan. Surrender is never easy. Our human nature fights against it, but as our relationship with God matures, then surrendering will not be so difficult. This is one reason why it is beneficial to surround ourselves with other Christians. The Bible says we are not to forsake the assembling of ourselves together, so that we can exhort one another, stir up love, and hold fast the confession of our hope. We all struggle with different areas of our walk and we should be encouraging each other to surrender more and grow through our trials of life. Sometimes we mess up God's plan when we get impatient and move without Him or when we doubt and sit still. God moves in many ways and every situation that arises in our life can teach us something valuable about our Christian walk.

Read Hebrews 10:19-25 and answer the questions below.

What encouragement do we get in verses 19-21 to strengthen our faith? _____
_____
_____
_____

How are we encouraged to go to God in verse 22? _____
_____
_____
_____

What does verse 23 say? _____
_____
_____
_____

What do verses 24 and 25 say we should do for one another? _____
_____
_____
_____

The assembling of ourselves together is usually done in a church setting on a Sunday Morning, Night and/or Wednesday Night. When we come together in the faith, we can learn from each other, but that will also take surrendering to listen and receive instruction or correction. Many say they don't have to go to church to be a Christian. This is true, but if we are Christians, we should want to be in church to feed our soul. *"And He Himself* (Jesus) *gave some to be apostles, some prophets, some evangelist, and some pastors and teachers, for the equipping of the saints for the work of ministry, for the edifying of the body of Christ, till we all come to the unity of the faith and the knowledge of the Son of God, to a perfect man, to the measure of the stature of the fullness of Christ; that we should no longer be children, tossed to and fro and carried about with every wind of doctrine, by the trickery of men, in the cunning craftiness by which they lie in wait to deceive, but, speaking the truth in love, may grow up in all things into Him who is the head – Christ – from whom the whole body, joined and knit together by what every joint supplies, according to the effective working by which every part does its share, causes growth of the body for the edifying of itself in love."* Ephesians 4:11-16. God has set men and women apart to teach His word and instruct others in the faith. This is the authority God has placed in our churches to guide us in His ways. It is important that we surrender to their authority because God has placed them there to teach us. So, going to church is important for our spiritual growth. *"Remember those who rule over (lead) you, who have spoken the word of God to you, whose faith follow, considering the outcome of their faith."* Hebrews 13:7. In following their faith, we will become mature Christians, strong in the faith, and surrender to the Father.

Read Romans 13:1-7 and answer the questions below.

What does verse 1 say about all authority? _____
_____
_____

What does verse 2 say about those who resist authority? _____
_____
_____

What does verse 3 say about good and evil? _____
_____
_____

What does verse 4 say about who the authority is? _____
_____
_____

What do verses 5-7 say our responsibilities are? _____

_____

_____

_____

_____

_____

Surrendering to the authorities in our life is expected, even as Christians. It is not a onetime thing. Just as repentance is a lifestyle, so is surrender. As the Lord shows us things in our life we need to change, we repent and surrender to His will. This is our maturing process; spiritual maturity takes time, surrender, repentance, and obedience. It is so easy for us to get impatient in our walk with God. We are just like little kids; we can't wait to grow up, we act older than we are, and we annoy others with our "adult" attitude. When we do this, it makes it difficult for us to be instructed because we think we already know it all. The truth is we are stubborn and rebellious, just like some teenagers, to the authority that God has placed before us to be taught.

Read 1 Corinthians 3:1-3 and answer the questions below.

What does Paul say about how he was able to speak to these people? _____

_____

_____

Why does he say that he was not able to feed them solid food? _____

_____

_____

For us to get from pure milk to solid food, we need someone of full age to instruct us. Jesus told Ananias in Acts 9:15 *"Go, for he* (Paul) *is a chosen vessel of Mine to bear My name before Gentiles, kings, and the children of Israel."* Paul instructed many Christians in the truth of God's word and God still has His servants today, set apart to teach us the truth of His word. *"Obey those who rule over you, and be submissive, for they watch out for your souls, as those who must give account. Let them do so with joy and not with grief, for that would be unprofitable for you."* Hebrews 13:17. The servants of the Lord should be obeyed, respected, and prayed for by us. They will stand before the Lord and give an account to Him for their job in feeding us. They need to know that we respect them enough to listen to their instructions and that we love them enough to lift them in prayer. We hinder our own growth when we refuse to surrender. As we feed on the pure milk of the word, receive correction from our pastors, and continually surrender more of our life, then our fellowship with the Father will grow us into strong, mature, and healthy Christians walking in the fear of the Lord.

Worship

Worship is our everyday life in a relationship of love. It is seen in our service to Him and must be in spirit and truth.

"For it is written, 'You shall worship the Lord your God, and Him only you shall serve."

Matthew   4:10

"God is Spirit, and those who worship Him must worship in spirit and truth."

John 4:24

Chapter 7 ~ Exaltations in Word

Exaltation requires expressions with the words of our mouth. Expressions are the part of our conversation where we share our feelings in the relationship. We use these expressions to tell about our love to others and our thankfulness for them. We use words to describe how we feel about what they say and do. Our words are needed in our relationships, so they can understand how we feel and we can understand how they feel. The Bible says, *"For what man knows the things of a man except the spirit of the man which is in him?"* 1 Corinthians 2:11. It is impossible for us to know how a person feels unless they share it with their words. We have all been in situations where people in our life act a certain way around us and we have wondered if they like us or not. Until they let it be known by speaking it, we always question. Words that express the heart are very important in our relationships and our relationship with God is no different.

Read Philippians 4:4-7 and answer the questions below.

What does it say about how to speak in verse 4? _____
_____
_____

What does it say in verse 5 about our speech? _____
_____
_____

What does verse 6 say about what we say? _____
_____

What is the benefit in verse 7? _____
_____

There are benefits to spending time with God and our relationship with Him will be seen in how we speak. We have to use our words to receive Jesus as our Lord and Savior. *"For whoever calls upon the name of the Lord shall be saved."* Romans 10:13. *"If you confess with your mouth the Lord Jesus and believe in your heart that God has raised Him from the dead, you will be saved. For with the heart one believes to righteousness, and with the mouth confession is made to salvation."* Romans 10:9-10. The words of our mouth are very important because it shows our salvation. With salvation, we come into the sheepfold and begin our relationship with the Father.

Read John 10:25-30 and answer the questions below.

What does Jesus say about the sheep in verse 27? _____

_____

_____

We have to use our words to stay in a relationship with Him. This is prayer and is necessary to grow closer to God and His will for our life. *"Therefore by Him let us continually offer the sacrifice of praise to God, that is, the fruit of our lips, giving thanks to His name."* Hebrews 13:15. Spending time with God is a privilege we often take for granted, but if we will be faithful with our time, we will find a Father, Comforter, and Friend. However, this does not give us the right to take advantage of God's goodness, He is still God, and we should honor Him as such.

Read Ecclesiastes 5:2-7 and answer the questions below.

What does verse 2 say about our mouth, heart, and words? _____

_____

_____

What does verse 3 say? _____

_____

_____

How does verse 4 and 5 refer to our words? _____

_____

_____

What does verse 6 say that our mouth causes us to do? _____

_____

_____

What warning do we find in verse 7? _____

_____

_____

Our words can bless us or curse us, not because we have great power in our words, as some are teaching, but because our words can cause us to sin against God. The "name it and claim it" teaches people that all they have to do is confess things and they will possess them. So, we have people confessing money, cars, houses and other possessions. They are confessing that they have a million dollars as they live on welfare, and confessing that they have a Mercedes as they drive a Pinto, and that they live in a mansion as they call a shack their home. They get sick with a cold, headache or the flu and say, "I'm not sick in Jesus name" as they cough, sneeze, and throw up. They use the phrase "In Jesus Name" as magician's uses "abracadabra." The name of Jesus is holy because the one in whom the name belongs is holy. So, what about John 14:14, some may be asking, *"If you shall ask any thing in My name, I will do it"*? The consistent teaching with this Scripture is that Jesus is bringing understanding of how the Holy Spirit will give us the ability to go directly to the Father in Jesus name. Until now, they have asked nothing in Jesus name because He has not fulfilled prophesy at this time in Scripture. *"You did not choose Me, but I chose you and appointed you that you should go and bear fruit, and that your fruit should remain, that whatever you ask the Father in My name He may give you."* John 15:16. We don't want to claim this Scripture because it requires something of us; that we bear fruit and it remains. The fruit we should be bearing is that of the Spirit, *"...love, joy, peace, kindness, goodness, gentleness, faithfulness, longsuffering, and self-control..."* Galatians 5:22-25.

Read John 15:1-11 and answer the questions below.

Who is the branch? _____

What does He do to help the branch bear much fruit? _____

What does that mean? _____

What happens if a branch does not abide in the Vine? _____

What does verse 7 say? _____
_____
_____
_____

What does verse 8 say? _____
_____
_____
_____

What must we do to abide according to verse 10? _____

The branch must be connected and stay connected to the vine according to verse 6. The only way to get connected is to receive Jesus Christ as our Lord and Savior. The Bible says that our confession is made unto salvation, Romans 10:10 not stuff. Our mouth will confess Jesus Christ or deny Him. *"Therefore whoever confesses me before men, him I will also confess before My Father who is in heaven. But whoever denies Me before men, him I will also deny before My*

Father who is in heaven." Matthew 10:32-33. Denying Jesus with our words only shows our lack of a relationship with Him. The choice of words we use to talk to God is ours, and how we talk to others is our choice, but the consequences of our words are up to God. Deny Jesus and He will deny us; that's what His word says, and that is what He means. *"For he is not a Jew who is one outwardly, nor is that circumcision which is outward in the flesh; but he is a Jew who is one inwardly, and circumcision is that of the heart, in the Spirit, and not in the letter; whose praise is not from men but from God."* Romans 2:28-29. Inward circumcision is of the heart, in the Spirit, where God sees. Man can't see in the heart, so whom are we trying to impress? If we claim Christ when around other believers, but hold our tongue around non-believers, then how will they come to know Christ if we are not sharing the gospel with them? *"How then shall they call on Him in whom they have not believed? And how shall they believe in Him of whom they have not heard? And how shall they hear without a preacher?"* Romans 10:14. The word preacher here means one who cries out publically or proclaims. Are we proclaiming Jesus, or are we proclaiming stuff?

Whatever we proclaim is what we are worshiping in our life. When we express our love to God, our gratitude for Jesus, or our testimony of a changed life, we are exalting God. All through the Bible, there are examples of how people expressed their love and gratitude to God. But King David's expressions are the greatest examples of all. In everything David did, he exalted God. *"I will love You, O Lord, my strength. The Lord is my rock and my fortress and my deliverer; my God, my strength, in whom I will trust; my shield and the horn of my salvation, my stronghold."* Psalm 18:1-2. *"The Lord lives! Blessed be my Rock! Let the God of my salvation be exalted."* Psalm 18:46. *"To You, O Lord, I lift up my soul. O my God, I trust in You."* Psalm 25:1-2. *"I will extol You, O Lord, for You have lifted me up."* Psalm 30:1. *"I will bless the Lord at all times; His praise shall continually be in my mouth."* Psalm 34:1.

He instructs others to exalt God in the same way. *"Give unto the Lord, O you mighty ones; give unto the Lord glory and strength. Give unto the Lord the glory due to His name; worship the Lord in the beauty of holiness."* Psalm 29:1-2. *"Oh, clap your hands, all you peoples! Shout to God with the voice of triumph! For the Lord Most High is awesome; He is a great King over all the earth."* Psalm 47:1-2. *"Rejoice in the Lord, O you righteous! For praise from the upright is beautiful."* Psalm 33:1. *"Great is the Lord, and greatly to be praised"* Psalm 48:1. *"Make a joyful shout to God, all the earth! Sing out the honor of His name; make His praise glorious. Say to God, How awesome are Your works! Through the greatness of Your power Your enemies shall submit themselves to You. All the earth shall worship You and sing praises to You; they shall sing praises to Your name."* Psalm 66:1-4.

These are only a few of many expressions that David extended to God showing his love by exalting Him. Even when David felt alone or scared, he cried out to God with praise. *"Save me, O God, by Your name, and vindicate me by Your strength."* Psalm 54:1. *"Whenever I am afraid, I will trust in You. In God (I will praise His word), in God I have put my trust; I will not fear. What can flesh do to me?"* Psalm 56:3-4. When David prayed, he exalted God continually throughout the prayer. Of all the kings who had done evil in the sight of God, David is the only one who repented. It is no wonder God said he was a man after His own heart. With everything David did, he extended praise to God. When he repented of his sins in Psalm 51, everything was still about God. *"Have mercy upon me, O God, according to Your lovingkindness."* (verse1) *"Against You, You only, have I sinned, and done this evil in Your sight."* (verse4) *"O Lord, open my lips, and my mouth shall show forth Your praise"* (verse 15). David did not lack in showing forth praise and worship to God. He should be an example to all of us, of how to exalt the God of our salvation. This is not about asking God for anything, it is simply thanking Him for what He has already done, believing in what He is going to do, and knowing whom He is. That is worship and its reason enough to exalt God with our tongue. We can take some lessons from David and learn to exalt God in every situation even when we are corrected and need to repent.

Exaltation requires expressions in deeds with our conduct. When we express exaltations, it is done with the words of our mouth and shown by our conduct. This is how we bear fruit. When we say that we forgive someone, our conduct should show that forgiveness. When we say thank-you to someone, our conduct should show that thankfulness. As parents, we know how it feels when our kids are ungrateful for the things that we give to them and are unthankful for the sacrifices we had to make to give it. They halfheartedly say thank-you, but their actions show that they are not thankful at all. They are just glad they got what they wanted and they know that's the thing to say. It breaks our heart and makes us feel as if we are raising bratty kids. Most of us don't want our kids to grow up with an expectant attitude, but a grateful one. God feels the same way about us. We have all probably been guilty of giving Him a thank-you with our lips but not showing thank you with our conduct. Have we really been thankful for the things God has done for us? Are we truly grateful for the sacrifice He made to give it to us? Can we truly be happy that we have eternal life? Is what Jesus did on the cross enough for us to be happy? If so, then exalting the Lord in word and deed should not be a problem. Expressions of love and gratitude should be heard from our mouth and seen in our conduct otherwise, we are hypocrites. Our mouth should not contradict our conduct because actions speak louder than words. So, whatever we say that we believe will be confirmed by our actions. However, our actions will tell the truth of what we believe, if they do not match our words then we are hypocrites.

Jesus gives us many very good descriptions of a hypocrite or pretender in Matthew chapter 23. If we look at the chapter, several verse; 13, 14, 15, 23, 25, 27, and 29 say, *"woe to you, scribes and Pharisees, hypocrites!"* This was the religious people of Jesus' day. He called them hypocrites because their words contradicted their deeds. Christians today are also labeled as hypocrites. Not all Christians are hypocrites, but the ones who do not live what they say they believe have not just given Christianity a bad name, but also God. *"For the name of God is blasphemed among the Gentiles because of you."* Romans 2:24. Who is causing God to be blasphemed? Those who make their boast in the law, with their lips, but break the law that they boast in, through their deeds cause God to be blasphemed, verse 23. The same is true of us today, making boasts that we are Christians, but breaking all the commands in our deeds. If we claim to be a Christian because we said a prayer and go to church, but we do not live as Christ, then we are a hypocrite.

The term Christian means follower of Christ. The definition of a Christian is a person who adheres to the life and teachings of Jesus Christ. If we follow Christ and adhere to His teachings, then we will live a Christian life. Many people claim Christianity without understanding what it means to be a Christian. The Bible gives us many verses of Scripture to help us on our journey with God in the Christian life. *"I beseech you therefore, brethren, by the mercies of God, that you present your bodies a living sacrifice, holy, acceptable to God, which is your reasonable service. And do not be conformed to this world, but be transformed by the renewing of your mind, that you may prove what is that good and acceptable and perfect will of God."* Romans 12:1-2. *"Therefore, having these promises, beloved, let us cleanse ourselves from all filthiness of the flesh and spirit, perfecting holiness in the fear of God."* 1 Corinthians 7:1. *"Therefore gird up the loins of your mind, be sober, and rest your hope fully upon the grace that is to be brought to you at the revelation of Jesus Christ; as obedient children, not conforming yourselves to the former lusts, as in your ignorance."* 1 Peter 1:13-14 says. *"Let this mind be in you which was also in Christ Jesus."* Philippians 2:5. It is up to us to follow Jesus and to adhere to His teachings. It is all about a choice, not to just confess Him with our lips, but to let Him be seen as we live our life in a Christ-like manner. Church attendance does not qualify us as Christians. Claiming the morals and values of Christianity does not qualify us as Christians. The only thing that qualifies us as Christians is to follow and adhere to Jesus Christ. The disciples were not called Christians because they attended church or because they were good men. They were called Christians because they followed the teachings of Jesus and taught others to follow Him too. A consistent lifestyle is a must to be a Christian. *"But be doers of the word, and not hearers only, deceiving yourselves."* James 1:22.

Read Ephesians 5:1-11 and answer the questions below.

What does verse 1 say we should do if we are children? _____
_____
_____

What Christ-like conduct should we be imitating in verse 2? _____
_____
_____

What should not be named among the saints in verse 3? _____
_____
_____

What things are not fitting in verse 4? _____
_____
_____

Who has no inheritance in the kingdom of Christ and God according to verse 5? __

_____

_____

The wrath of God comes because of what things, in verse 6? _____

_____

_____

We are given some instruction and guidance in verses 6 and 7. Let no one deceive you and do not be partakers with these people.   What other instructions do verses 8, 9, 10, and 11 give to Christians? _____

_____

_____

_____

_____

We expose darkness by living in the light of Christ Jesus, walking in the fruit of the Spirit, and having our fellowship in the truth of God, proving what is acceptable to the Lord. We don't find any exceptions for people who said a prayer or go to church. *"Do you not know that the unrighteous will not inherit the kingdom of God? Do not be deceived. Neither fornicators, nor idolaters, nor adulterers, nor homosexuals, nor sodomites, nor thieves, nor covetous, nor drunkards, nor revilers, nor extortioners will inherit the kingdom of God."* 1 Corinthians 6:9-10. It doesn't say that we can be any one of these things as long as we say a prayer or go to church.   These kinds of people are in the church, calling themselves Christians, believing they are going to heaven, but they are deceived. Paul writes, *"I wrote to you in my epistle not to keep company with sexually immoral people. Yet I certainly did not mean with the sexually immoral people of this world, or with the covetous, or extortioners, or idolaters, since then you would need to go out of the world. But now I have written to you not to keep company with anyone named a brother, who is a fornicator, or covetous, or an idolater, or a reviler, or a drunkard, or an extortioner – not even to eat with such a person."* 1 Corinthians 5:9-11.

Unfortunately, we have it all backwards just as the Corinthians did. We exclude ourselves from people we could be a witness to and hang out with people that are "Christians" in name only. We think we have a Christian friend, but their words and deeds contradict each other. Maybe we have even questioned their salvation, then felt bad because who are we to say if someone is saved or not. John 7:24 says, *"Do not judge according to appearance,* (well, they go to church, they say they are a Christian) *but judge with righteous judgment* (is their conduct righteous)." If they do not conduct themselves in a Christ-like manner then they are not a Christian. This is not to say that we receive salvation through our works, certainly not! *"For by grace you have been saved through faith, and that not of yourselves; it is the gift of God, not of works, lest anyone should boast."* Ephesians 2:8-9. However, verse 10 goes on to say, *"For we are His workmanship, created in Christ Jesus for good works, which God prepared beforehand that we should walk in them."* If we hang out with those who only claim Christianity, but doesn't walk in the good works, we may find ourselves acting just like them. *"He who walks with wise men will be wise, but the companion of fools will be destroyed."* Proverbs 13:20. As true Christians, we need to choose our friends wisely and expose darkness by being the light, even to people who claim to be Christians but prove differently by the contradiction of their words with their deeds.

In being a Christian friend, it is also our responsibility to correct when we see our Christian friends getting off the path of righteousness. *"Brethren, if anyone among you wanders from the truth, and someone turns him back, let him know that he who turns a sinner from the error of his way will save a soul from death and cover a multitude of sins."* James 5:19-20. This saying is backed up in 1 Peter 4:8, *"And above all things have fervent love for one another, for love will cover a multitude of sins."* This does not mean that we should hide their sin for them so that they can stay in sin, but that we will correct them with truth so they can repent and be set free from it. *"Rebuke a wise man, and he will love you. Give instruction to a wise man, and he will be still wiser; teach a just man, and he will increase in learning. The fear of the Lord is the beginning of wisdom, and the knowledge of the Holy One is understanding."* Proverbs 9:8-10. If they are true Christians, they will be grateful for your love, repent from their sin, and thank you for helping them back.

Read Romans 2:5-13 and answer the questions below.

What do we have to look forward to if we have a hard, unrepentant heart? _____
_____
_____

God will render to each one of us according to our what? _____
_____
_____

What do verses 7 and 10 say? _____
_____
_____

What do verses 8 and 9 say? _____
_____
_____

Who is justified according to verse 13? _____

_____

_____

Consistency is the key to living a Christian life. We express with our words the greatness of God. We express with our deeds that we believe in the greatness of God. Our words and deeds work together to show our faith in our Lord and Savior. *"What does it profit, my brethren, if someone says he has faith but does not have works? Can faith save him? If a brother or sister is naked and destitute of daily food, and one of you says to them, 'Depart in peace, be warmed and filled,' but you do not give them the things which are needed for the body, what does it profit? Thus also faith by itself, if it does not have works, is dead. But someone will say, 'You have faith, and I have works.' Show me your faith without your works and I will show you my faith by my works."* James 2:14-18. If we have faith in God, it will be seen in our conduct, deeds, and works, which all show an outward action of our faith and prove our relationship with the Father.

Exaltation requires expressions of our testimony. A testimony is a declaration. We declare to others the experiences of our day, the experience on our vacation, or the overall experience of a particular job. A testimony is a declaration of our life changing experience with God. Our testimony is very important in our Christian life. *"And they overcame him (Satan) by the blood of the Lamb and by the word of their testimony, and they did not love their lives to the death."* Revelation 12:11. Without the testimony of the Apostles, we would not have the testimony of Jesus Christ with us today. The testimony of Jesus is what brought us to salvation, strengthens our faith, and gives us hope. As we share our testimony with others about our changed life with Christ, the testimony of Jesus is continued as they receive and give their testimony to others. *"And this is the testimony: that God has given us eternal life, and this life is in His Son. He who has the Son has life; he who does not have the Son of God does not have life. These things I have written to you who believe in the name of the Son of God, that you may know that you have eternal life, and that you may continue to believe in the name of the Son of God."* 1 John 5:11-13. The great thing about the testimony of Jesus is that we become beneficiaries when we receive it and as we share with others, they can become beneficiaries too.

When we express the wonderful works God has done in our life, we express a testimony of His goodness. Acts 2:11 says that people from all different dialects heard the wonderful works of God when the Holy Spirit came down on the day of Pentecost. Then Peter preaches a sermon full of power, love, and truth. He says to them, *"Repent, and let every one of you be baptized in the name of Jesus Christ for the remission of sins; and you shall receive the gift of the Holy Spirit."* (vs. 38) *"And with many other words he testified and exhorted them, saying, 'Be saved from this perverse generation.' Then those who gladly received his word were baptized; and that day about three thousand souls were added to them."* (vs. 40-41) Repentance is the key to receiving a testimony. When we repent or ask God to forgive us with no intentions of practicing sin anymore, then we begin to think differently, talk differently, and act differently. When this happens, people around us notice the difference, and that is a testimony. None of us is perfect, we will all make mistakes, battle sin, and sometimes fall down, but we can strive to do better each day of our life, so that others can see Christ in us and desire Him.

Read Psalm 51:6-13 and answer the question below.

Where does God seek for us to be honest according to verse 6? _____

_____

_____

What evidence do we have of David's faith in verse 7? _____

_____

_____

How do verses 9 and 10 show David's repentant heart? _____

_____

_____

What shows David's desire for God in verses 11 and 12? _____

_____

_____

What evidence do we have in verse 13 that David will use his testimony to win the lost? _____

_____

_____

David did not intend to hide his changed life, the sin he had been delivered from, or the God that did it all. David goes on to say, *"The sacrifices of God are a broken spirit, a broken and contrite heart – these, O God, You will not despise."* Psalm 51:17. This is a condition of the heart, where God sees. Honesty, faith, repentance, and desire for God brings us to a place that we can exalt God in our testimony. We should never be ashamed of what God has done for us, no matter how bad we think we have been. We should use it for His glory that others may glorify Him too. It doesn't matter what we have done, nothing is so horrible that it will keep us from God if we come to Him with a repentant heart. David took another man's wife, got her pregnant, and killed her husband, but he repented. He could then use his life as a testimony of God's love and forgiveness.

Read 1 Timothy 1:12-15 and answer the questions below.

Whom does he thank for his life in verse 12? _____

What do we see about Paul in verse 13? _____

_____

_____

_____

What does he reaffirm about Jesus in verses 14 and 15? _____

_____

_____

_____

How does verse 16 display a testimony for others? _____
_____
_____

Whom does he glorify in verse 17? _____
_____
_____

Paul consented to the death of Stephen (Acts 8:1), made havoc of the church, threw men and women into prison (Acts 8:3), and breathed threats of murder against the disciples (Acts 9:1). He was not a quiet sinner that wasn't noticed much, he made a negative impact on many lives. However, he repented in Act 9:6 when he said, *"Lord, what do You want me to do?"* He surrendered his life to the will of God and lived his life as a testimony for Jesus Christ from that day forward. He knew what kind of man he had been, the sins he had committed, and he knew who gave him mercy and grace to be set free. In Act 26, he gives his testimony to King Agrippa, among others, and verse 28 says, *"Then Agrippa said to Paul, 'You almost persuade me to become a Christian."* That is what our testimony is all about, to share the greatness of God, His love, grace, and mercy, and give them hope in Christ Jesus. *"Therefore, as the elect of God, holy and beloved, put on tender mercies, kindness, humility, meekness, long-suffering; bearing with one another, and forgiving one another, if anyone has a complaint against another; even as Christ forgave you, so you also must do. But above all these things put on love, which is the bond of perfection. And let the peace of God rule in your hearts, to which also you were called in one body; and be thankful. Let the word of Christ dwell in you richly in all wisdom, teaching and admonishing one another in psalms and hymns and spiritual songs, singing with grace in your hearts to the Lord. And whatever you do in word or deed, do all in the name of the Lord Jesus, giving thanks to God the Father through Him."* Colossians 3:12-17.

Discipline

Discipline is a lifestyle of obedience for a Christian. We are disciplined by God and in turn, we have to discipline ourselves. It is the only way to become more Christ-like.

"And also if anyone competes in athletics, he is not crowned unless he competes according to the rules."

2 Timothy 2:5

"But I discipline my body and bring it into subjection, lest, when I have preached to others, I myself should become disqualified."

1 Corinthians 9:27

Application requires an attitude of humility. Humility is not a strong suit for human beings. We are more likely to be prideful in some situations than we are to be humble. However, humility is a necessity for a Christian. It is commanded by God, *"He has shown you, O man, what is good; and what does the Lord require of you but to do justly, to love mercy, and to walk humbly with your God?"* Micah 6:8. When we walk with God in humility, and He will lift us up. *"Humble yourselves in the sight of the Lord, and He will lift you up."* James 4:10. When we walk with God in humility, He will honor us. *"Before destruction the heart of a man is haughty, and before honor is humility."* Proverbs 18:12. When we walk with God in humility, He will hear our prayers. *"If my people who are called by My name will humble themselves, and pray and seek My face, and turn from their wicked ways, then I will hear from heaven, and will forgive their sin and heal their land."* 2 Chronicles 7:14. When we walk with God in humility, He will exalt us, *"For whoever exalts himself will be humbled, and he who humbles himself will be exalted."* Luke 14:11. Time and time again, throughout Scripture, we find blessings for our humility. *"Lord, You have heard the desire of the humble; You will prepare their heart; You will cause Your ear to hear."* Psalm 10:17. We can expect wonderful things from God, if we walk in humility.

We lose so much of God's goodness that He wants to give us, when we will not humble ourselves to Him. If we think about it, the only thing that keeps us from being humble is our pride. What exactly is pride that we would give up so many of God's blessings to keep it? Pride is an overly high opinion of oneself. Pride is thinking well of oneself. In each of these definitions, we have our "opinion" which is formed in our mind and we have "thinking" which is an action of our mind.

Read Philippians 2:1-11 and answer the questions below.

What does it say about our mind? _____

_____

_____

_____

_____

What description is given about pride? _____

_____

_____

_____

_____

What information do we receive about Christ's attitude? _____

_____

_____

_____

_____

What does God do as a result of His attitude? _____

_____

_____

_____

_____

God shows no partiality, just as He did for Jesus, He will do for us; exalt the humble. Jesus tells us to learn from Him. *"Take My yoke upon you and learn from Me, for I am meek and lowly in heart, and you will find rest for your souls."* Matthew 11:29. If we are to be Christ-like then that means that we also must be meek, this is humble. *"Now may the God of patience and comfort grant you to be like-minded toward one another, according to Christ Jesus, that you may with one mind and one mouth glorify the God and Father of our Lord Jesus Christ."* Romans 15:5-6. If all Christians were of a humble attitude, then the division of opinions would not get in the way of us all having the mind of Christ.

Pride keeps our mind from being changed from ourselves to God. Pride keeps us from hearing because we are wise in our own opinion. *"Be of the same mind toward one another. Do not set your mind on high things, but associate with the humble. Do not be wise in your own opinion."* Romans 12:16. Our prideful attitude keeps us from being of the same mind, the mind of Christ. What we think becomes more important than what God says. *"For whatever things were written before were written for our learning, that we through the patience and comfort of the Scriptures might have hope."* Romans 15:4. So, the things that are written in the Scriptures are for us to learn from, not to use to form our own opinions. Our opinions will not change God's word, nothing we can say, think, or feel will change what He said. What our opinion can do is get us into sin and away from God in all our ways.

Opinions say that God is not the same today as He was 40 years ago, or as He was in Jesus' day, or as He was in the Old Testament. However, God's word says, *"For I am the Lord, I do not change."* Malachi 3:6, *"Jesus Christ is the same yesterday, today, and forever."* Hebrews 13:8, *"God is not a man, that He should lie, nor a son of man, that He should repent. Has He said, and will He not do it? Or has He spoken, and will He not make it good?"* Numbers 23:19. God doesn't change, we do. We change how we want to hear God, what we want to receive from God, and we put God in a box where we are comfortable because of our pride. We don't want to admit we are wrong, we don't want to admit that we need to change, or even that maybe we have been a hypocrite; pretending to be someone that we are not.

Pride is an ugly attitude that will not only cause us to sin but will keep us in sin. It is sneaky and comes in many shapes and sizes. Pride can consume us to the point we do no wrong and keep us from hearing and receiving the gospel of Jesus Christ. Pride can also be in certain areas of our life and will keep us from surrendering our whole heart to Him. We can be prideful about the neatness of our house, the beautiful garden we planted, the way we raise our kids, and even how great we are to our spouse. Strangely enough, we can even be prideful about how kind and considerate we are. We must be so careful to keep ourselves clear of any pride, which is a continual battle, because it will creep in before we realize it. *"Pride goes before destruction, and a haughty spirit before a fall."* Proverbs 16:18. Sometimes things are falling apart in our life because of pride. *"When pride comes, then comes shame; but with the humble is wisdom."* Proverbs 11:2. When we are corrected we may feel ashamed, then we get offended, but that is just pride. Feeling offended is a natural, human response, however, how we respond to our offence will determine if we will stay in our sin or gain wisdom. It's all about our attitude of pride or humility.

Pride is not a little thing that we should not take notice of, it is very serious. *"Everyone who is proud in heart is an abomination to the Lord; though they join forces, none will go unpunished."* Proverbs 16:5. If our relationship with the Lord means anything to us, then this should scare us enough to check our heart to see if we have any pride in it anywhere. *"The fear of the Lord is to hate evil; pride and arrogance and the evil way and the perverse mouth I hate."* Proverbs 8:13. We say, "God is so loving, giving, and caring, He doesn't hate," this is our opinion. His word says that He hates pride, arrogance, perverse mouth, and evil ways. We have to be so careful not to form our opinion of God based on pieces of Scripture, man's doctrine, or an experience we've had. Otherwise, we will be so set on our opinion of what we think that we will not hear the truth of the word of God. If we will humble our heart and decide that we are not all knowing, accept that we could be wrong, and listen, we will hear and understand.

Read Proverbs 4:1-9 and answer the questions below.

Refer verse 1 with Psalm 34:11. What does it say about our learning as children? _

_____

_____

What do you see about humility and wisdom when referencing this Scripture with Proverbs 11:2? _____

_____

What do you see about the fear of the Lord and wisdom when referencing this Scripture with Proverbs 9:10? _____

_____

_____

If we will let down our pride, humble our heart, receive our correction, instruction, and rebuke, we will find the fear of the Lord and begin to gain wisdom. God wants us to be, *"...filled with the knowledge of His will in all wisdom and spiritual understanding; that you may have a walk worthy of the Lord, fully pleasing Him, being fruitful in every good work and increasing in the knowledge of God; strengthened with all might, according to His glorious power, for all patience and longsuffering with joy; giving thanks to the Father who has qualified us to be partakers of the inheritance of the saints in the light."* Colossians 1:9-12. However, to receive all of this, we must first have a humble heart.

Application requires an attitude of obedience. In this relationship with the Father, there is an expectation of obedience just as our parents expected us to obey them and we expect our children to obey us. It is our responsibility as parents to teach our children. *"Train up a child in the way he should go, and when he is old he will not depart from it."* Proverbs 22:6. With all that society has become, it is easy to give our responsibility away to others. We don't have to teach our children to read and write because teachers at school do that. We don't have to teach our children the Bible because teachers at church do that. We don't have to teach our children about sex because kids at school do that. We don't have to teach our children anything because the world around us is doing it. Our children should go to school and get an education beyond what we can give. They should go to church and learn more about the Bible, just as we should. They will learn from other kids regardless of what we want, that can't be stopped. However, with all they learn in this world, it is still our responsibility to teach them the truth. Just because they may know what Jenny and Johnny say about sex, it is still important for us to have the "sex talk" to be sure they know the truth. School and Church should be a team effort between teacher and parent, so our children will be successful not only in their education, but also in their walk with God.

Our walk with God should be the most important thing in our life. When we understand our place as children, then we can better understand how to walk with God in the relationship. We want to claim great blessings and privileges without understanding the fullness of what we claim. Jesus said, *"No longer do I call you servants, for a servant does not know what his master is doing; but I have called you friends, for all things that I heard from My Father I have made known to you."* John 15:15. We want to say that God is my friend, but if we jump back one verse to John 15:14, we will see the big "if". *"You are My friends if you do whatever I command you."* Abraham was called a friend of God because he believed and obeyed. Obedience is a must to have the privilege of being called a friend. We want all the good things of God without all the commandments that go along with it. We want to claim Christianity without the obedience that goes with the lifestyle. *"...Shall we continue in sin that grace may abound? Certainly not! How shall we who died to sin live any longer in it?"* Romans 6:1-2. We can't just take the pieces of the Christian life that feel good. Christianity is a life of discipline. *"But to the wicked God says: What right have you to declare My statutes, or take My covenant in your mouth, seeing you hate instruction and cast My words behind you?"* Psalm 50:16-17.

To be obedient to God means that sometimes we will be corrected. We don't really like this is a part of our Christian life, because it doesn't feel good. We are grown adults, gone from under the authority of our parents, and have become "our own boss" so to speak. The thought of being "told what to do" causes us to think we will lose our identity. This may be true to some degree because Jesus said, *"...whoever loses his life for My sake will find it."* Matthew 16:25. However, being in obedience to the Father has its great rewards, but we have to endure some chastening to receive them. *"If you endure chastening, God deals with you as with sons; for what son is there whom a father does not chasten? But if you are without chastening, of which all have become partakers, then you are illegitimate and not sons. Furthermore, we have had human fathers who corrected us, and we paid them respect. Shall we not much more readily be in subjection to the Father of spirits and live? For they (fathers) indeed for a few days chastened us as seemed best to them, but He for our profit, that we may be partakers of His holiness."* Hebrews 12:7-10. God loves us so much that He will correct us, but do we love Him enough to submit our life to Him and obey?

Read Proverbs 3:1-12 and answer the questions below.

What does verse 1 tell us to do with God's law and commands? _____
_____
_____
_____

What is the result of obeying verse one? _____
_____
_____
_____

What does verse 3 tell us to do with truth and mercy? _____
_____
_____
_____

In verse 4, what do we need to do to find favor and high esteem in the sight of God and man? _____
_____
_____
_____

We are to do what according to verses 5 and 6? _____
_____
_____

Which part of verse 7 describes pride? _____

Which part of verse 7 describes humility? _____

What is verse 8 referring to? _____

In verses 9-10, what is God saying to you personally, about what you give? _____
_____
_____
_____
_____

What is the instruction that we receive from God in verse 11? _____
_____
_____
_____

What encouragement do we receive from God in verse 12? _____
_____
_____
_____

Just as children are disciplined by the authority in their lives, we must also become under the authority of God. Take a moment to examine your life, and ask God if you have rejected any of His corrections or teachings. If so, ask Him to forgive you for being a spoiled child and to show you how to receive what He has for you. Write out a prayer to help you apply it with a new attitude. _____
_____
_____
_____
_____
_____

If we apply these principles to our Christian life, we will find success in our relationship with the Father. It is not just the pastor's responsibility to teach us God's word. It is our responsibility to obey the teachings of His word. *"He who has My commandments and keeps them, it is he who loves Me. And he who loves Me will be loved by My Father, and I will love him and manifest Myself to him."* John 14:21. To keep His commandments means that we must obey them. *"...Behold, to obey is better than sacrifice, and to heed than the fat of rams. For rebellion is as the sin of witchcraft, and stubbornness is as iniquity and idolatry."* 1 Samuel 15:22-23.

There's an old saying, "You can lead a horse to water, but you can't make him drink." This is true for us as Christians. The pastor can bring food from heaven for us to eat, but he can't make us eat it. His job is to obey God to feed us, but it is our job to obey God and eat. The key is obedience. Our pastor can open all the spiritual doors of heaven to bring understanding, but we still have to make the choice to walk in. If we will walk in with a humble and obedient attitude, willing to repent, then we will find a healthy Christian life, full of love, joy, and peace. We won't be perfect; we are human beings and will always wrestle our flesh for as long as we live, but we can make it with a repentant heart.

Read Romans 1:18-25 and answer the questions below.

Verse 18 describes people who do *what* to the truth? _____

How do they do that according to verse 19? _____
_____
_____

What does verse 20 say about God? _____
_____
_____

Who is "they" in verse 20? _____
_____
_____

What does verse 21 say? _____
_____
_____

What did they profess with their mouth according to verse 22? _____

What did they glorify instead of God in verse 23? _____
_____
_____

What resulted in their lives because they would not confess and live what they knew to be true in verse 24? _____
_____
_____

What exchanges and compromises did they make according to verse 25? _____
_____

These eight verses are a description of a people who knew the truth of God, but would not obey that truth, because they refused to repent. Paul says in Act 17:30 that God calls all men everywhere to repent. However, before we will have a repentant heart we must first have a humble heart. In humility, we will see our faults and ask for forgiveness, which is repentance. We should never think that we don't need to change. The wrath of God will be against us with that attitude. Perfection has not arrived for any of us, but we are to *"grow in the grace and knowledge of our Lord and Savior Jesus Christ."* 2 Peter 3:18. The only way we can grow is if we listen and obey. *"Therefore, my beloved brethren, let every man be swift to hear, slow to speak, slow to wrath; for the wrath of man does not produce the righteousness of God. Therefore lay aside all filthiness and overflow of wickedness, and receive with meekness* (humility) *the implanted word, which is able to save your souls. But be doers of the word, and not hearers only, deceiving yourselves."* James 1:19-22. When we hear and receive the word with a repentant heart, then we are able to be a doer of the word. This is where humility and repentance go hand in hand to bring us to obedience.

Respect

Respect is our testimony of truth, love, worship, and discipline. When we recognize God, then we will have reverence for Him.

"I beseech you therefore, brethren, by the mercies of God, that you present your bodies a living sacrifice, holy, acceptable to God, which is your reasonable service."

Romans 12:1

"Sanctify yourselves therefore, and be holy, for I am the Lord your God. And you shall keep My statutes, and perform them: I am the Lord who sanctifies you."

Leviticus 20:7-8

Reverence requires recognition of God's appearance. The question of "what does God look like" has probably crossed our mind at least once in our lifetime. When we say, "look", we think with our eyes, a physical appearance. We have some physical descriptions of God in His word. In Daniel 7:9, we have a description of His hair and garments. *"And the Ancient of Days was seated; His garment was white as snow, and the hair of His head was like pure wool."* In Revelation 1:14-15 we have a little more detail. *"His head and His hair were white like wool, as white as snow, and His eyes like a flame of fire; His feet were like fine brass, as if refined in a furnace, and His voice as the sound of many waters; He had in His right hand seven stars, out of His mouth went a sharp two-edged sword, and His countenance was like the sun shining in its strength."* This is quite a description but doesn't answer our question. Genesis 1:27 says that God created man in His own image. We find in Joshua 5:13-15, that God came to Joshua in the appearance of a man. In Genesis 32:24-30, Jacob says he has seen God, but gives us no physical description of Him. Moses asks in Exodus 33:18, *"Please, show me Your glory."* God replied in verse 20, *"You cannot see My face; for no man shall see Me, and live."* So, we may be tempted to say that God looks like a man, but what about Exodus 13:21, God was before His people in a pillar of cloud during the day, and a pillar of fire at night. What about John 4:24, Jesus said, *"God is Spirit, and those who worship Him must worship in spirit and truth."*

So, with all this information we are still no closer to knowing what God looks like physically. That is because God does not put emphasis on the physical appearance of man and we should not put our emphasis on the physical appearance of God. *"But the Lord said to Samuel, 'Do not look at his appearance or at the height of his stature, because I have refused him. For the Lord does not see as man sees; for man looks at the outward appearance, but the Lord looks at the heart.'"* 1 Samuel 16:7. God knows what we think before we say it. He knows how we feel before we express it. He knows our intentions even when we try to hide them, because He knows our heart. *"I, the Lord, search the heart, I test the mind, even to give every man according to his ways, and according to the fruit of his doings."* Jeremiah 17:10. We choose the outcome of our life. We don't choose by having a title of ministry. We don't choose by how often we go to church, or how many duties we perform in the community, but we choose with what is in our heart. Physical always seems to get in the way of the Spiritual things that God wants to do in our life. We need to learn to see the way God sees, with spiritual eyes.

God is not like us. He doesn't look like us, act like us, or think like us. Just as His word cannot be read as if it were a typical book, neither can God be seen as if He were a typical man. We want to bring God down to our level of comprehension so we can feel better about our heart condition. Too many people are trying to understand and explain every detail of why God said, what God did, or how God works. *"For My thoughts are not your thoughts, nor are your ways My ways, says the Lord. For as the heavens are higher than the earth, so are My ways higher than your ways, and My thoughts than your thoughts."* Isaiah 55:8-9. We want to dig out the Bible as if its purpose is to be a history book. We tear it to pieces looking for all the symbolisms and hidden meanings. We analyze it to death, trying to figure out God with our brain. God is like nothing we can comprehend with our own human understanding. *"But the natural man does not receive the things of the Spirit of God, for they are foolishness to him; nor can he know them because they are spiritually discerned."* 1 Corinthians 1:14. None of our own knowledge or understanding can comprehend God. If we would stop trying to comprehend Him and just walk with Him in the fear of the Lord, we will gain wisdom that only He can give, and an understanding that is beyond human thinking.

We cannot allow these thoughts and ideas of God get us distracted from living our life with Him. Even as we go through this Bible Study, some may be tempted to dig out some historical fact, which only takes from the purpose of this study. We don't have to know all the mysteries of God to recognize Him when He appears in our life. Some people may say that we just need to have some common sense, morals, and values to see God. Others may say they see God every day in nature, or in people. This may all be true, but without the Holy Spirit, reverence will not come with the recognition. If the Holy Spirit abides in us, when we recognize God, then we will also revere Him.

Read Genesis 18:1-5 and answer the questions below.

According to verse 1, who appeared to Abraham? _____
_____
_____

What is Abraham's attitude when he sees the men? _____
_____
_____

What does Abraham say to them in verse 3? _____
_____
_____

What does he offer them in verses 4 and 5? _____
_____

Where does it say that Abraham was told that this was the Lord? It doesn't say it anywhere because no one told him. Abraham recognized God when He appeared and his response was to revere Him. This displays an attitude of one who has a relationship with God. If we are truly walking in the fear of the Lord, then when God appears, we will revere Him as the Lord. Reverence is hardly seen anymore because we are so conditioned to the rituals of the things of God. We determine how God will work in our future based on how He has worked in our past or how He worked things out for Sister Susie. God doesn't show partiality with what He gives, but how He appears in our life will not always be the same as before or the same as He appeared in someone else's life. We are individuals, with our own relationship, and as we grow in that relationship, God will appear to us differently. We have been guilty of placing God in a box of rules and routines that we can understand and comprehend.

We organize our day in a routine, so we have time to get things accomplished. We organize our duties at home and work, so that at the end of the day we can be finished. Organization is not a bad thing, but it has become such a way of life for us that we tend to organize God too. We organize our church services in a routine. When we walk in the door, we are handed a paper that lists the order of service. We sing three songs, have prayer, sing two more songs, the preacher gives a word, sing another song, have prayer, and then we go home. Nowhere on the list does it say, wait for God to appear or watch for God to appear. God can still appear in services put together this way, but many times the routine keeps us from recognizing Him when He does appear.

Some may say that God lives in them, so He is with them all the time and they take Him everywhere they go. Just because the Holy Spirit lives in us, does not mean that everything we do is God. Here again, God is not like us. We almost get numb to the things of God, not expecting Him to appear in any other way than what we are able to physically see or mentally comprehend. When we do see Him appear, we don't recognize that it's God and cheat Him of the reverence He is due. We say, "God can still do miracles", but if they are not something we think are miraculous, then we don't give Him praise. He very much wants us to see Him appear in our life because He is appearing; we just don't recognize and revere Him when He does.

Read John 8:31-44 and answer the questions below.

What attitude is displayed from the people who claimed to know God? _____
_____
_____

What did Jesus reveal about their heart in verses 34-37? _____
_____
_____

What does Jesus say to them in verse 38? _____

_____

_____

According to this passage, whom did they recognize and revere? _____

_____

_____

God was standing right before them and they didn't recognize Him because they didn't have a relationship with Him. They didn't understand His speech because they didn't know His voice. They hated His actions because it condemned their actions. Just because we go to church or call ourselves Christians does not mean we really have a relationship with Him. We recognize the people we have a relationship with; we know their walk, talk, and stature. We are familiar with their actions and attitudes; how they respond to situations and deal with feelings. This is the recognition we should have with the Father. We hear His voice, follow His commands, and respect His authority. We know how He will respond to our sin, our attitude, and our repentance. We know all of this, not because we go to church, claim Christianity, or do good deeds, but because of a relationship. God may appear in our life through the mouth of our children, the words of our pastor, or the actions of a friend. Let's not be like the Pharisees and miss God when He appears, but let's recognize and revere Him through a relationship.

Reverence requires recognition of God's natural attributes. Attributes are defined as a quality regarded as a characteristic or inherent part of someone. The attributes of God are whatever God has revealed about Himself as being true. It is not a part of God; it is how He is and what He is. These are not qualities God possesses; they are His very essence. God's attributes do not change, die or diminish. The natural attributes of God cannot be obtained by us. We do not have these characteristics, and God will never ask us to strive for them. These are what come with being the one true God.

God is Omniscient, which is all-knowing. God knows the very intent of our hearts; the reason we do what we do (Hebrews 4:12). He knows what we need before we ask (Matthew 6:8), and knows the desire of our heart (Psalm 37:4). *"Great is our Lord, and mighty in power; His understanding is infinite."* Psalm 147:8. We cannot comprehend the infinite knowledge of God by our own understanding. He is immutable; never changes. When we were kids, what we wanted to be when we grew up changed many times before we decided. Our desire changes, our mind changes, and our attitude changes, so to understand that God doesn't change is hard to comprehend. However, God feels the same way about sin today as He did in David and Solomon's day, no matter what we say. He is absolutely unchangeable whether we like it or not. *"For I am the Lord, I do not change..."* Malachi 3:6. We cannot comprehend the knowledge of God or His unchanging Spirit, but do we recognize it?

Read Psalm 130:1-6 and answer the question below.

What evidence do you see of His Omniscience? _____
_____
_____
_____

God is Omnipresent, which means present everywhere. Proverbs 15:3 says, *"The eyes of the Lord are in every place, keeping watch on the evil and the good."* As the creator, He watches over His creation, limitless to any bounds. He cares about His creation and He has promised to always be with us. *I will never leave you nor forsake you* (Hebrews 13:5, Deuteronomy 31:6). God is infinite; not limited or contained to any space. We understand shapes and sizes. We don't try to put a horse in the front seat of our car because we analyze the size of the horse and the space it needs. For us to comprehend the size of God that He fits nowhere, but is everywhere doesn't make logical sense to us. Solomon expresses to God in 1

Kings 8:27, *"But will God indeed dwell on earth? Behold, heaven and the heaven of heavens cannot contain You. How much less this temple which I have built!"* He is eternal; the absences of time. We understand time as past, present, and future, but Revelation 1:8 says, *"I am the Alpha and the Omega, the Beginning and the End, says the Lord, who is and who was and who is to come, the Almighty."* He is not confined to time but is everlasting. *"Lord, You have been our dwelling place in all generations. Before the mountains were brought forth, or ever You had formed the earth and the world, even from everlasting to everlasting, You are God."* Psalm 90:1-2. His presence is all around us at all times, but do we recognize it?

Read Psalm 139:7-13 and answer the question below.

What evidence do you see of His Omnipresence? _____
_____
_____
_____

God is Omnipotent, which means has all power. Nothing is impossible for God. (Luke 18:27). He is the great power that causes the sun to rise in the morning and set in the evening. He's the One that tells the stars to shine, the One that channels the waters and turns the earth. *"And He has made from one blood every nation of men to dwell on all the face of the earth, and has determined their pre-appointed times and the boundaries of their dwellings."* Acts 17:26 He made the plants to produce oxygen to feed our blood, and food to feed our bodies. All things around us were created by God. He gives breath and life to every living creature and purpose for all things made. He is sovereign; the absolute authority. He is accountable to no one or thing. He does as He pleases but He will not contradict His other attributes. *"The Lord kills and makes alive; He brings down to the grave and brings up. The Lord makes poor and makes rich; brings low and lifts up."* I Samuel 2:6-7. His power is all around us, but do we recognize it?

Read Jeremiah 32:17-19 and answer the question below.

What evidence do you see of His Omnipotence? _____
_____
_____
_____

"God, who made the world and everything in it, since He is Lord of heaven and earth, does not dwell in temples made with hands. Nor is He worshiped with men's hands, as though He needed anything, since He gives to all life, breath, and all things." Acts 17:24-25. He is self-existent; *"For as the Father has life in Himself,*

so He has granted the Son to have life in Himself." John 5:26. God told Moses, *"I AM*

WHO I AM. Thus you shall say to the children of Israel, I AM has sent me to you." Exodus 3:14. He is self-sufficient; *"If I were hungry, I would not tell you; for the world is Mine, and all its fullness."* Psalm 50:12. It is because of the natural attributes of God that we are even in existence. When we know His attributes, we can better recognize how big He is and how small we are. However, we don't have to understand or comprehend these attributes to recognize God; we just need to accept that they are God.

Reverence requires recognition of God's moral attributes. This moral character makes up whom God is. Once again, these are not qualities God possesses; they are His very essence. God's attributes do not change, die, or diminish. Unlike His natural attributes, the moral attributes of God can be obtained by us. We do not have these characteristics naturally, as He does, but are commanded to strive for them. These are qualities that are expected from the children of the one true God.

God is Holy. This describes God's purity. He is free from all evil doing; perfect and sinless. *"For I am the Lord your God, the Holy One of Israel, your Savior."* Isaiah 43:3. He commanded the children of Israel to be holy, just as He is holy. *"For I am the Lord who brings you up out of the land of Egypt, to be your God. You shall therefore be holy, for I am holy."* Leviticus 11:45. God doesn't change so He expects the same of us today.

Read 1 Peter 1:13-16 and answer the questions below.

What does it say about our holiness? _____
_____
_____
_____

What does it say about our obedience? _____
_____
_____
_____

What does verse 16 say? _____
_____
_____
_____

God is Righteous. This describes His perfect acts of goodness. The things He does are righteous because He is righteous. *"The righteousness of God which is through faith in Jesus Christ to all and on all who believe."* Romans 3:22. We obtain righteousness only through the faith of Jesus Christ. *"Little children, let no one deceive you. He who practices righteousness is righteous, just as He is righteous."* 1 John 3:7.

Read Philippians 3:8-10 and answer the questions below.

What does it say about our righteousness? _____
_____
_____
_____

What does it say about the righteousness of God? _____
_____
_____
_____

What does it say that we gain? _____
_____
_____
_____

God is Justice. He never has punished His creatures wrongly and He never will. He is just in all His ways. *"And if you call on the Father, who without partiality judges according to each one's work, conduct yourselves throughout the time of your sojourning here in fear."* 1 Peter 1:17.

Read 2 Thessalonians 1:5-10 and answer the questions below.

What kind of judgment does it say God has? _____
_____
_____
_____

Whom does it say God takes vengeance on? _____
_____
_____
_____

What does verse nine say about those who do not obey? _____
_____
_____
_____

God is Mercy. God has compassion on the obedient and the disobedient. His active compassion is what keeps us from getting what we deserve according to our iniquity. *"For judgment is without mercy to the one who has shown no mercy. Mercy triumphs over judgment."* James 2:13.

Read Matthew 18:23-35 and answer the questions below.

What is the lesson of this parable? _____
_____
_____
_____

What do verses 34-35 say? _____
_____
_____
_____

What is the key phrase in verse 35? _____
_____
_____
_____

God is Love. God is the very definition of love that is described in 1 Corinthians 13:4-8, 14:1 says that we should pursue love. If God is love then He is whom we should be pursuing. *"My little children, let us not love in word or in tongue, but in deed and in truth."* 1 John 3:18.

Read 1 John 4:7-21 and answer the questions below.

What are we commanded to do in these verses? _____
_____
_____
_____

What fact is stated about love in these verses? _____
_____
_____
_____

What consistencies about love are in these verses? _____
_____
_____
_____

"Whoever does not practice righteousness is not of God, nor is he who does not love." 1 John 3:10. *"Do not judge according to appearance, but judge with a righteous judgment."* John 7:24. *"Blessed are the merciful, for they shall obtain mercy."* Matthew 5:7. *"But as He who called you is holy, you also be holy in all your*

conduct." 1 Peter 1:15. These are commands that God expects from His children. Nowhere in God's word does it say that Christianity is an easy life, that we will be loved by all, or that all our problems would go away. Nowhere in God's word does it say that we can say a prayer and not change. God commands holy living, righteous acts, merciful hearts, righteous judgment, and to love our brother.

God gives us free will to choose to obey or reject, but not the freedom to negotiate the results of that choice; that is determined by His sovereign will. When we give up our own will and surrender to His will, then He can bless our life, but He will not bless sin or those who practice it. *"Not everyone who says to Me, 'Lord, Lord,' shall enter the kingdom of heaven, but he who does the will of My Father in heaven. Many will say to Me in that day, 'Lord, Lord, have we not prophesied in You name, cast out demons in Your name, and done many wonders in Your name?' And then I will declare to them, 'I never knew you; depart from Me, you who practice lawlessness!'"* Matthew 7:21-23. *"Do you not know that the unrighteous will not inherit the kingdom of God? Do not be deceived. Neither fornicators, nor idolaters, nor adulterers, nor homosexuals, nor sodomites, nor thieves, nor covetous, nor drunkards, nor revilers, nor extortioners will inherit the kingdom of God."* 1 Corinthians 6:9-10. *"It is a fearful thing to fall into the hands of the living God."* Hebrews 10:31. *"For God did not call us to uncleanness, but in holiness. Therefore he who rejects this does not reject man, but God, who has also given us His Holy Spirit."* 1 Thessalonians 4:7.

Chapter 15 ~ Spirit

Reverence requires recognition of God's Spirit. The fruits of the Spirit are the result of God's moral attributes, which are to be our moral attributes if we are of Christ. There is an expectation to obtain these attributes and the fruit of those attributes be seen in our life. God does not expect us to achieve this on our own; He gives us everything we need to succeed in a Christian life. He would not command us to do something that was impossible to obtain. He gives us the ability through the Holy Spirit to do all things. *"I say then: 'Walk in the Spirit, and you shall not fulfill the lust of the flesh. For the flesh lusts against the Spirit, and the Spirit against the flesh; and these are contrary to one another, so that you do not do the things that you wish. But if you are led by the Spirit, you are not under the law.'"* Galatians 5:16-18.

Read Galatians 5:19-26 and answer the questions below.

What are the works of the flesh? _____
_____
_____

What does it say will happen if we practice living in the flesh? _____
_____
_____

What are the fruits of the Spirit? _____
_____
_____

What does it say that we should do to our flesh? _____
_____
_____

Read Romans 8:4-11 and answer the questions below.

What does it say about the flesh? _____
_____

What does it say about the Spirit? _____
_____
_____

Having this information should help us to see our heart. The wrestle of the Spirit and flesh will continue till the day we die. Sometimes we will show a work of the flesh in our life, but that in and of itself will not get us in trouble with God. What gets us in trouble is the practicing of these works, which will separate us from God. However, if we will repent, which shows the fruit of the Spirit, God is faithful to forgive us. *"If we confess our sins, He is faithful and just to forgive us our sins and to cleanse us from all unrighteousness."* 1 John 1:9. This does not give us a free ticket to sin, with the intentions of asking for forgiveness. This is willful sinning and God knows when we do it. *"For if we sin willfully after we have received the knowledge of the truth, there no longer remains a sacrifice for sins, but a certain fearful expectation of judgment, and fiery indignation which will devour the adversaries."* Hebrews 10:26-27. Verse 29 explains that when we willingly sin, we trample the Son of God underfoot, count His blood a common thing, and insult the Spirit of grace. *"For we know Him who said, 'Vengeance is Mine, I will repay' says the Lord. And again, 'The Lord will judge His people.' It is a fearful thing to fall into the hands of the living God."* Hebrews 10:30-31. This is also a part of the fear of the Lord, to know that He is just and repay our iniquities. *"And do not fear those who kill the body but cannot kill the soul. But rather fear Him who is able to destroy both soul and body in hell."* Matthew 10:28. *"In mercy and truth atonement is provided for iniquity; and by the fear of the Lord one departs from evil."* Proverbs 16:6. If we have a relationship, in the fear of the Lord, we will not want to hurt our Lord by walking against Him. Christianity is a lifestyle of discipline because of love in a relationship.

Read 2 Peter 1:3-8 and answer the questions below.

What has His power given to us? _____
_____
_____

What have we been given to be partakers of? _____
_____
_____

What should we add to our faith? _____
_____
_____

What promise is given if we abound in these things? _____
_____
_____

_____

When the Holy Spirit dwells in us, we will recognize the Spirit of God around us. We will be drawn to it and desire to be with those who possess it. The Holy Spirit is our Helper so we can become all that God has created us to be, live according to His word, and walk in the fear of the Lord. *"In the fear of the Lord there is strong confidence, and His children will have a place of refuge. The fear of the Lord is a fountain of life, to avoid the snares of death."* Proverbs 14:26-27. God does not call us to be perfect but to, *"...pursue what is good both for yourselves and for all. Rejoice always, pray without ceasing, in everything give thanks; for this is the will of God in Christ Jesus for you. Do not quench the Spirit. Do not despise prophecies. Test all things; hold fast what is good. Abstain from every form of evil. Now may the God of peace Himself sanctify you completely; and may your whole spirit, soul, and body be preserved blameless at the coming of our Lord Jesus Christ. He who calls you is faithful, who also will do it."* (1 Thessalonians 5:15-24)

Read Psalm 25:12-14 and answer the questions below.

Who is taught in the way of the Lord? _____

Who shall dwell in prosperity? _____

Whose descendants shall inherit the earth? _____

The secret of the Lord is with whom? _____

To whom will He show His covenant? _____

When we delight in the fear of the Lord, then we are a delight to the Lord. *"The Lord takes pleasure in those who fear Him, in those who hope in His mercy."* Psalm 147:11. The fear of the Lord is the key to our Christian life, and when we walk in it, we will find our life closer to Him.

~Conclusion ~

Thank you for taking the time to work through this study. I pray it has helped you grow closer to the Father in a relationship. I hope you have been encouraged and been given a more in-depth understanding of the fear of the Lord. As you live each day, remember to faithfully fellowship with your heavenly Father. Give Him expressions of exaltations out of love from your heart. Be thankful for the corrections and instructions so that you can apply His teachings with a good attitude. Recognize when God is working in your life, revere whom He is, and respect His authority in your life. I learned so much about how to have a true, intimate, fulfilling relationship through writing this study. I pray that your life is forever changed to know truth, give love, display worship, receive discipline, and show respect to God.